Introduct...

This guide features f...
walks in the Souther...
Galloway Hills, Lowtl...
Clyde and Tweed, Edi...
and the Cheviot and Langholm Hills.

Routes have been chosen according to a number of factors, including variety of terrain, great views, historical interest, minimal road walking and the feasibility of a circular route.

Environmental factors such as the ability of access points to support additional cars and opportunities for bypassing visitor-sensitive or eroded areas have also been taken into account. Circular routes help to take the pressure off badly eroded paths, and walking in areas where there have been fewer footsteps is more conducive to natural regeneration of the land. Walkers are also encouraged to take variations from the walks described, where terrain and experience allow.

Walkers can minimise their own impact on the environment by using purpose-built paths whenever possible and walking in single file to help prevent widening scars. Restricting your use of bikes to designated tracks, parking sensibly, using stiles and gates where they exist (and never crossing tensed wire fences), avoiding fires and litter, and keeping dogs on a tight lead, particularly on grazing land and during lambing, all help to preserve the land and good relations with its inhabitants. Many of the responsibilities for walkers are now enshrined in law.

...'re divided into five ...largely represent points of access into the mountains, or use natural geographical boundaries. The opening section for each of the five regions introduces the area, its towns, topography and key features, and contains brief route outlines. It is supplemented by a road map, locating the walks.

Each route begins with an introduction identifying the names and heights of significant tops, the relevant Ordnance Survey (OS) map, total distance and average time.

A sketch map shows the main topographical details of the area and the route. The map is intended only to give the reader an idea of the terrain, and should not be followed for navigation.

Every route has an estimated round-trip time: this is for rough guidance only and should help in planning, especially when daylight hours are limited. In winter or after heavy rain, extra time should also be added for difficulties underfoot.

Risks and how to avoid them

Many of the hills in this guide are remote and craggy, and the weather in Scotland can change suddenly, reducing visibility to several yards. Winter walking brings particular challenges, including limited daylight, white-outs, cornices and avalanches. Every year, walkers and climbers die from falls or hypothermia in the Scottish mountains. Equally, though, overstretched Mountain Rescue teams are often called out to walkers who are simply tired or hungry.

Preparation for a walk should begin well before you set out, and your choice of route should reflect your fitness, the conditions underfoot and the regional weather forecasts.

None of the walks in this guide should be attempted without the relevant OS Map or equivalent at 1:50,000 (or 1:25,000) and a compass.

Even in summer, warm, waterproof clothing is advisable and footwear that is comfortable and supportive with good grips is a must. Don't underestimate how much food and water you need and remember to take any medication required, including reserves in case of illness or delay. Many walkers also carry a whistle, first aid kit and survival bag.

It is a good idea to leave a route description with a friend or relative in case a genuine emergency arises: you should not rely on a mobile phone to get you out of difficulty. If walking as part of a group, make sure your companions are aware of any medical conditions and how to deal with problems that may occur.

There is a route for most levels of fitness in this guide, but it is important to know your limitations. Even for an experienced walker, colds, aches and pains can turn an easy walk into an ordeal.

These routes assume some knowledge of navigation in the hills with use of map and compass, though these skills are not difficult to learn. Use of Global Positioning System (GPS) devices is becoming more common but, while GPS can help pinpoint your location on the map in zero visibility, it cannot tell you where to go next.

Techniques such as scrambling or climbing on rock, snow and ice are required on only a few mountains in this guide. Such skills will improve confidence and the ease with which any route can be completed. They will also help you to avoid or escape potentially dangerous areas if you lose your way. The Mountaineering Council of Scotland provides training and information.

For most of these routes, proficiency in walking and map-reading is sufficient.

Access

Until the Land Reform (Scotland) Act was introduced early in 2003, the 'right to roam' in Scotland was a result of continued negotiations between government bodies, interest groups and landowners.

In many respects, the Act simply reinforces the strong tradition of public access to the countryside of Scotland for recreational purposes. However, a key difference is that under the Act the right of access depends on whether it is exercised responsibly.

Landowners also have an obligation not to unreasonably prevent or deter those seeking access. The responsibilities of the public and land managers are set out in the Scottish Outdoor Access Code.

At certain times of the year there are special restrictions, both at low level and on the hills, and these should be respected. These often concern farming, shooting and forest activities: if you are in any doubt, ask. Signs are usually posted at popular access points with details: there should be no expectation of a right of access to all places at all times.

The right of access does not extend to use of motor vehicles on private or estate roads.

Seasonal restrictions
Red deer stalking:
Stags: 1 July to 20 October
Hinds: 21 October to 15 February
Deer may also be culled at other times for welfare reasons. The seasons for Roe deer (less common) are also longer.
Grouse shooting:
12 August to 10 December
Forestry:
Felling: all year
Planting: November to May
Heather burning:
September to April
Lambing:
March to May (Dogs should be kept on a lead at all times near livestock.)

Glossary
Common Scots and Gaelic words found in the text and maps:

bealach (Gaelic)	pass; gap; gorge
brae	slope; hills
bucht	sheepfold
cairn	pile of stones
cleuch, cleugh	gorge; ravine; cliff
close	enclosed farmyard
coomb	mountain hollow; corrie
craig	crag; rocky place
dod, dodd	rounded hill
dyke	wall
flow, flowe	peat bog
gairy	steep hill; precipice
grain	branch of a burn or glen
hope	haven; mountain hollow
kip, kipp	peak; projecting point
kirk	church
knowe	knoll; hillock; hillside
lane	marshy meadow; burn
law	rounded hill
linn	steep watercourse
lochan (Gaelic)	small loch; pool
mains	home farm of an estate
mere	pool; pond
nick	narrow gap in hills; notch
rig	ridge; section of a field
shank	slope or projecting point
slack; slock	hollow between hills

Dumfries and Galloway is a county of many guises. Travelling inland from the coast, lush farmland gives way to some rough topography. In the Galloway Forest

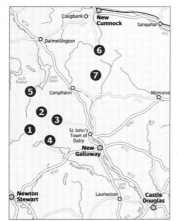

Park, lochs sprawl across the quag and the wild crags have even wilder names. The aura of wilderness continues north to the fringes of Ayrshire, before the land descends to the rolling plain of the West Central Belt. A mountain bike is a good asset in the Galloway Hills: an extensive system of trails winds through the forests, making this a world-class mountain bike venue.

In this section, two routes start from Glen Trool: one climbs the giant of Merrick, the other takes in a lower peak with some tough walking. A circuit, best accessed by bike, begins by Clatteringshaws Loch. The long sweeping ridge of the Rhinns of Kells, above St John's Town of Dalry, is the target for a fourth walk. Loch Doon is the access point for a long march to the shores of Loch Enoch. Further east, the rounded knolls above Afton Water give a half-day route, and the remoter Cairnsmore of Carsphairn is approached from the south.

The Galloway Hills

① Rig of the Jarkness   8
Strenuous, half-day route along a charismatic ridge deep in
the Galloway Hills

② Merrick and the Grey Man   10
Test your navigation skills with this challenging ascent of Merrick
over undulating and often boggy terrain

③ Rhinns of Kells   12
Fine ridge joining the hills of Meikle Millyea and Corserine with
good mountain paths, pleasant forest tracks and great views

④ A Curleywee Circuit   14
Varied walk requiring good navigation skills over Lamachan Hill
and Curleywee. A bike is recommended for the approach

⑤ Mullwharchar Marathon   16
Challenging walk around Loch Enoch in wild country with
fine views and a quiet return beside the river. Stamina essential

⑥ Sweet Afton   18
Easy half-day circuit on the rounded, windswept ridges above
Glen Afton, with views which inspired Robert Burns

⑦ Cairnsmore of Carsphairn   20
Varied route over several peaks with steep climbs rewarded
by fine views to the Galloway Hills, and one river crossing

Rig of the Jarkness

Craiglee (531m)

Walk time 3h40 Height gain 450m
Distance 11km OS Map Landranger 77

This walk follows a watercourse and old paths over some arduous terrain to reach a fine ridge with great views of the surrounding hills.

Start at the end of the public road and parking area above Loch Trool (GR415803). Take a gravel track east past Bruce's Stone, losing some height. Walk past the turning to Buchan, across a stile and along the track towards Glenhead. At a junction about 100m before the house, take the right fork to descend towards a bridge over Glenhead

Burn. Immediately before the bridge, take the waymarked Southern Upland Way to follow the water on its north bank. Just after climbing a stile, cross a burn by stepping stones and gain height easily to reach Trostan Burn. Leave the path here and follow the water upstream. In dry conditions this provides a delightful way up, with slabs and boulders to aid progress. Away from the rocks the walking is arduous, a taste of the terrain to come. Continue east, keeping to the high ground as much as possible, but the ground is boggy and clumpy, requiring real stamina. This leads to the tiered rock bands, which can be easily negotiated to reach the summit and trig point of Craiglee

(GR462801) (2h20). Follow the ridge northwest on much firmer terrain, where a path meanders over granite slabs and twists between outcrops and hidden lochans. Now walk along the rounded Rig of the Jarkness. When the ridge becomes less defined and the terrain becomes more difficult, descend north over heather to reach Loch Valley. Follow the angler's path west to the foot of the loch and cross the Gairland Burn to join another path. Follow this path southwest, losing height steadily above the glen. Contour around the ridge to join a wall that takes you to a gate. Go through this and descend through thick heather. Another two gates lead down to the original track near Buchan, leaving only a short stroll back to the start (3h40).

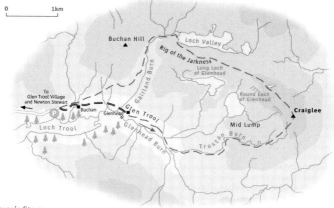

Bruce's Stone

The huge stone at the head of Loch Trool is a granite reminder of Robert the Bruce's victory over the English in March 1307 when he cleverly isolated and ambushed a force of 2000 troops on the 'Steps o'Trool'. Having landed at Carrick with limited support a few weeks earlier only to find that two of his brothers had been beheaded, Bruce had little option but to revert to such guerilla tactics. His shrewd leadership won him a popular following, however, as he gradually extended a campaign which was 'brought to a decisive close' at Bannockburn seven years later.

◄ Loch Trool and Mulldonoch from Bruce's Stone

Merrick and the Grey Man

Buchan Hill (493m), **Merrick** (843m)

Walk time 6h20 Height gain 900m
Distance 16km OS Map Landranger 77

A popular mountain taken by two of its less-visited ridges, with some steep but avoidable sections and plenty of arduous terrain. Stamina and navigation skills are essential for this route.

Start at the end of the public road and parking area above Loch Trool (GR415803). Walk east along the gravel track, losing height. Pass a turning for the house of Buchan on the right and watch for a gate on the left 50m further on. Go through this and take the path, which cuts through the heather close to the east bank of Buchan Burn. After passing through a second gate,

aim for the bulk of the crags on Buchan Hill as you climb NNE to arrive at a static gate. Climb over this and bear north towards the leftmost crags above. The path weaves a clever line through the candy-striped rocks to gain the top of Buchan Hill, its three summits marked with large cairns. A good path now takes you northwards over the highest ground of Rig of Loch Enoch, requiring lots of ups and downs but no technical difficulty. Eventually this leads to Craig Neldricken, overlooking Loch Enoch [Escape: descend southwest to reach the plantation, then follow the route instructions at the end to return to Loch Trool.] Keep to the western edge of the loch to reach a wall at the northwest tip. Follow the wall over difficult and boggy ground for

◄ The Grey Man of Merrick and Benyellary

about 1km. Above lies the imposing northeast corrie of Merrick. The ridge on the right hand side of the corrie looks intimidating, but the ascent between broken buttresses to the top of Little Spear is steep rather than difficult. [Variant: to avoid this, continue to Loch Twachtan, climb heathery slopes to gain the bealach shared with Kirriereoch Hill and ascend Little Spear.] This leaves only a short climb south to the summit of Merrick (GR427855) (4h). Descend ESE onto Redstone Rig and follow the folded ridge down to a bealach above the southwest tip of Loch Enoch. Walk southwest for about 300m, and watch for the curious rock feature known as the Grey Man of Merrick on your right. Cross the fence and follow it down to the top of a plantation. Continue your descent close to the Buchan Burn on the east side of the trees until there is a break in the forest and two burns converge. Turn into the plantation, cross the burn and walk along the west bank for about 1km. On reaching some posts, climb right to find the end of a gravel track above. Follow this and watch for the intersecting path close to a bridge after 500m, then turn left along the path to reach a ruined cottage and preserved carving. Walk southwards through the trees, along the burn and back to the start (6h20).

The Awful Hand

The Merrick is the highest mountain in southern Scotland and, according to Sheriff Nicolson of Skye, a Gaelic scholar, it is the 'highest knuckle of the hand' which this hill grouping resembles, as *meurach* means branched or fingered in Gaelic. Later writers dubbed the range 'The Awful Hand' as it can be a rough and forbidding place, 'not yet approved of God' as Galloway writer S R Crockett put it.

Rhinns of Kells

Meikle Millyea (746m), **Corserine** (814m)

Walk time 6h + detour 1h
Height gain 900m Distance 16km
OS Map Landranger 77

A steep start to an exhilarating ridge walk that features two larger Galloway peaks, with a short detour to reach a cairn with historic connections.

Start at the end of the public road and car park in the clearing just before Forrest Lodge (GR552862). From the clearing, walk southwest on Prof Hans Heiberg Road, a good forest track. Pass the house at Burnhead and continue southwest, passing through two gates and ignoring the turn-off

for Mary Watson Road. Carry straight on at the crossroads with Kristin Olsen Road and follow the Prof's track as it performs several turns towards the edge of the fenced plantation. The track divides shortly after passing a watchtower. Take the left turn (west) and look out for a path on the left after about 40m. This leads to a stile after 100m. Cross this to exit the plantation. Cross this to exit the plantation, and accompany the fence westwards over rough ground. After about 200m, strike diagonally southwest up the craggy slopes of Meikle Lump. The easiest way to the ridge follows a watercourse through clumpy heather by old fenceposts. Once on the ridge, a path takes you over

◀ The Rhinns of Kells from Mullwharchar

A cairn for a King

Carlin's Cairn on the hill to the north of Corserine is one of the biggest in the south of Scotland and, according to legend, dates back to the time of Robert the Bruce. It is said to have been built by a miller's wife in gratitude for land given to her by the Bruce, after she had helped to shelter him prior to his victory over the English at Glen Trool in 1307. The names of other nearby sites, such as the King's Well, also commemorate the three months he spent as an outlaw in the Galloway Hills.

alternating boggy and rocky sections to the summit of Meikle Millyea (GR518828) (2h20). Descend NNW to begin a fine walk along the main ridge of this massif. An old wall leads you down to a boggy area with many lochans. Continue over the bumpy knolls of Milldown and Millfire with views to Silver Flowe, heavily forested on its east side, and boasting some of Galloway's most treacherous bog to the west. A long uphill march leads you to the summit of Corserine (GR498870) (4h20). [Detour: Descend

northwards to the bealach and up to Carlin's Cairn. Return the same way (1h).] Walk east over the plateau for about 500m and bear northeast towards Polmaddy Gairy. Rather than taking the north ridge, drop eastwards to follow a narrow path, keeping north above the east corrie that feeds Folk Burn. After about 1km, just north of Folk Burn and beyond a low crag with a prominent capped roof, a stile leads into the forest. Cross the stile to follow the path beside the burn to Birger Natvig Road. Turn right (southeast) and follow this main track, ignoring Robert Watson Road and other branches. This track takes you back to Forrest Lodge and the start (6h).

13

A Curleywee Circuit

Lamachan Hill (717m), **Curleywee** (674m)

Walk time 3h40 Height gain 450m
Approach and return 1h bike or 2h20 walk
Distance 10km + 10km approach and
return OS Map Landranger 77

**Great route over twin peaks and around
an atmospheric corrie in mountain
biking territory. This walk contains some
rough ground, and good navigation is
required in descent. Use of a bike will
save time at the start.**

Start at Craigencallie House, at the end of
the public road, west of Clatteringshaws
Loch (GR504779). (For an extended start by
bike, begin at the visitor centre on the

loch.) Walk or cycle north from the end of
the road on the gravel track. At the junction
after 1.5km, take the left fork and continue
as far as the White Laggan Burn, which
feeds into Loch Dee. Leave bikes here: walk
times start at this point. Continue
westwards along the track until it starts its
descent into Glen Trool. Leave the track
before a fence and wall on the left to
shadow a cascading burn. The ground is
particularly rough here, but the water is an
interesting distraction. When the ground
levels out after a short distance, trend WSW
over very boggy ground and then follow the
vague northeast ridge of Bennanbrack,
passing giant erratics, to reach the plateau.

◄ Loch Dee and Meikle Millyea

The summit of Lamachan Hill lies just to the west (GR435770) (2h20). Pass over the rocky top of Bennanbrack and take the exciting path above the corrie to a gap and wall below Curleywee. Climb easily to the summit for some fine views over the Galloway Forest. Descend carefully southwards: as well as low crags, there are very steep cliffs on the east face of the peak and the paths are ill defined. From the easier but complex ground shared with Bennan Hill, drop east to join an old path. Follow the path through several boggy sections to the plantation. Walk along the forest break to the bothy, close to the original track (3h40). Return to the start.

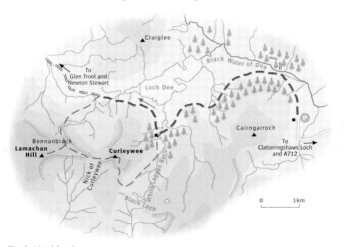

The Raiders' Road

Popularised by the writer Samuel Rutherford Crockett in his novel *The Raiders* (1894), a tale of Border intrigue and cattle reiving, this 16km (10-mile) forest road was the route once taken by drovers and raiders from New Galloway to Mossdale. The writer was born at nearby Little Duchrae Farm and a memorial at Laurieston, Clachanpluck in the novel, is inscribed with a tribute from Robert Louis Stevenson, with whom Crockett regularly corresponded.

Mullwharchar Marathon

Mullwharchar (692m)

Walk time 7h Height gain 500m
Distance 22km OS Map Landranger 77

A demanding route along an erratic-strewn ridge with views over Merrick and good tracks to access and return.

Start at the eastern end of the Forest Drive on Loch Doon, about 1km south of Loch Doon Castle (GR476942). Take the track southwards, go over the bridge and walk towards the head of the loch. Cross the bridge over the Gala Lane here, and watch for a track on the right just beyond. This winds through the forest, crossing one small bridge after 2km, where the track now becomes fainter and leads to a second bridge with fine views up to Craignaw. Cross the Gala Lane and walk west: when the track disappears, tramp over rough bog and ascend steep heather slopes to gain the firm north ridge of Hoodens Hill. Climb southwards beside giant erratics, liberally strewn across the ridge, to reach the top of the fell. Drop down to a rounded bealach to the south and climb gentle slopes and intermittent rocky terraces to the summit of Mullwharchar (GR453866) (3h20). Descend easily south to relax by the sandy shores of Loch Enoch, a good spot for lunch. Loop clockwise around the loch, passing under the rough flanks of Merrick,

and cross the fence at the northwest tip. Walk north to join Eglin Lane and follow this burn on its east side as it drops in lively cascades only to rest indolently in the glen below. This gives a hard tramp through the clumpy grasses, a real test of stamina and determination. After passing a rocky ravine close to the confluence with the Black Garpel, pass over an old fence to finally reach the footbridge. Go over this and climb through the forest

break to an intersection after 500m. Turn right and follow the forest track as it heads north and then west to reach a wider track. Turn right, cross the concrete bridge and walk to the Forest Drive. This leaves about 2km back to Loch Doon and the start (7h).

Castle Island

Built on a rocky islet at the southern end of Loch Doon in the late 13th century, Doon Castle was an odd-looking, eleven-sided stronghold which was besieged several times in its turbulent history. The ruins which can be seen today are those of the original castle which were relocated when the level of the loch was raised as part of the Galloway hydro-electric scheme in the 1930s. When the level of the loch is very low, however, it is still possible to see the top of what was once Castle Island.

Sweet Afton

Blackcraig Hill (700m),
Blacklorg Hill (681m)

Walk time 4h40 Height gain 600m
Distance 13km OS Map Landranger 77

**A peaceful route with plenty of bog but
splendid views, extensive signposting
and no navigation difficulties.**

Start at the turning for Blackcraig in Glen
Afton, about 5km south of New Cumnock
(GR631080). (Parking south towards the
reservoir.) Take the gravel track over the
bridge, bypassing the cottage at Blackcraig
by a gate on the left and gaining height
easily as you continue up the track.
Where the gravel turns to mud after about
500m, descend to the burn and follow
this upstream until it disappears.
Continue over boggier ground to reach
the flats of Quintin Knowe and the county
boundary. Follow the fence to climb
southwest up a blunt ridge. Where the
spur levels out, it is best to keep to the
highest ground a little way west of the
fence. A few low outcrops lead to the trig
point and summit of Blackcraig Hill
(GR647064) (2h20). Descend southwards,
rejoin the fence and follow this down over

grassy slopes to a boggy bealach. Now climb Greenlorg Hill to reach the top of Blacklorg Hill. Drop westwards on undulating heather by another fence, and climb Cannock Hill with its fine views over Afton Reservoir. Shadow the fence as you descend NNW to the bealach shared with Craigbraneoch Rig. Drop westwards down to a stony path near the edge of the reservoir. Follow this north to reach the dam, and roll down the grassy slopes to reach a track. Follow the track past the extensive waterworks and along Glen Afton to the start (4h40).

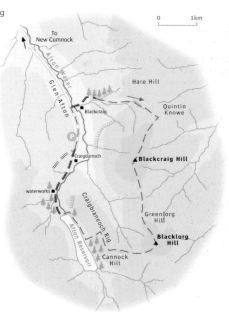

Sweet Afton

When Irish tobacco company P J Carroll thought to rebrand their popular pipe tobacco for the Scottish market they were struck by the fact that Robert Burns' sister, Agnes Burns-Galt, was buried in the cemetery near their Dundalk factory. Sweet Afton cigarettes, with a picture of the bard and the first lines of the poem written during his shepherding days on the packet, went on to become bestsellers. Seventies heavy rock band Black Sabbath later wrote the track *Sweet Leaf* as a tribute to their favourite cigarettes and not, as many critics thought at the time, marijuana.

◀ *Wind turbines on Hare Hill, above Glen Afton*

Cairnsmore of Carsphairn

Moorbrock Hill (650m),
Cairnsmore of Carsphairn (797m)

Walk time 6h Height gain 800m
Distance 16km OS Map Landranger 77

Some fine peaks reached over a mixture of tracks and rough ground, with bog and a river crossing to finish.

Start at the track marked for Moorbrock and Strahanna, 500m northeast of Craigengillan on the Water of Ken road, 11km east of Carsphairn (by road) (GR640953). (Minimal parking: do not block access or passing places.) Walk around the gateway and take the track that rises in zigzags, passing a watchtower to reach a junction of several tracks. Take the track in the centre to continue due north through forestry, with views of the steep face of Moorbrock Hill: it is worth approaching from this direction to plan your ascent. The track doubles back south, crossing Keoch Lane to reach a major forest break below the mountain. Leave the track here and climb beside a burn. Higher up, a narrow rib on the north bank takes you directly up to the main face. This is easier than it looks from below, with clumpy heather and scree leading up to a small buttress, arranged as a skewed 'i'. Pass this on the left (awkward) or further to the right to reach easy ground

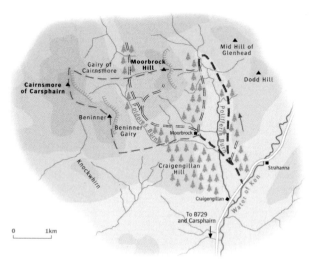

and the plateau of Moorbrock Hill beyond (GR620984) (2h20). [Escape: walk south along the plateau, and then join a good track which leads to the farm at Moorbrock.] Descend west over easy-angled slopes to a burn and follow this to cross a track, then walk over the quaggy bealach shared with Cairnsmore. Pass through one gate in the north-south fence and continue west on even slopes on the north side of the intersecting fence. Where this turns abruptly south at a large heptahedral block, continue straight on towards the east face. Keep right of a scree slope and ascend steepening slopes to reach the plateau, leaving only a short walk to the summit of Cairnsmore of Carsphairn (GR594979) (4h).

[Variant: for a gentler ascent, bear north under the face until it is easy to join the wide north ridge. Double back to the top.] Drop south, then southeast across a boulder-strewn terrain, pass over the stile at the bealach and march the short way to the top of Beninner. Follow the wide curve of the south ridge: there is no breach in the eastern corrie until you have reached the boggy flats. Walk east across the grain of ditches to reach Poldores Burn. Ford the water before reaching the plantation and follow the opposite bank downstream until you come to a meeting point of three walls. Accompany the wall on the left to reach the farm buildings at Moorbrock and a track that leads you back to the start (6h).

◀ Moorbrock Hill from the east

Between Scotland and England, the M74 snakes past forested slopes, and gives only a rare glimpse of the mountain landscape beyond. On the west side, the Lowthers first appear as undulating moorland, but further towards Galloway the high plateau is torn by ravines and arched ridges. The Moffat Hills are more consistently rolling, but they hide deep corries and high waterfalls. The Tweed begins its journey here and a scattering of Victorian reservoirs have helped shape a different landscape.

In the Lowthers, two contrasting routes commence in old mining villages: a multi-top trek from Wanlockhead, and a half-day walk over Green Lowther from Leadhills. The celebrated Dalveen Pass holds centrestage for a round of several peaks and the reclusive Queensberry tempts lovers of moorland with far-reaching views. Over in the Moffat Hills, Hart Fell makes an excellent objective from the haunting Devil's Beef Tub and the quiet parish of Tweedsmuir is the setting for an unusual walk above Talla Reservoir. Broad Law makes for a challenge from Megget Reservoir, whilst the tops behind St Mary's Loch give an easier circuit which begins by Tibbie Shiels Inn. Lastly, a climb by the Grey Mare's Tail starts a route over White Coomb.

Lowther and Moffat Hills

1 **Wanlockhead's Treasures** 24
Long circuit that climbs many small hills, returning by the
mineral-rich Wanlock Water. Stamina essential

2 **Mists of Green Lowther** 26
Shorter route over rough ground and by watercourses to climb
Green Lowther high up in gold-panning country

3 **Steygail and Lowther Hill** 28
Exhilarating circuit of many peaks around the celebrated
Dalveen Pass, with plenty of rough walking but fantastic views

4 **Queensberry Rules** 30
A hard climb by ravines and meandering burns to Queensberry
which, on a fine day, rewards with views of the Lakes

5 **The Devil's Beef Tub and Hart Fell** 32
Ridge walk featuring Hart Fell with a great aspect into the
corries and a series of small ascents over its neighbours

6 **Tweedsmuir and Talla** 34
Epic journey high above Talla Reservoir with some extreme
gradients and a fine forestry trail to finish

7 **Broad Law over Megget** 36
Strenuous circuit which climbs the lofty Broad Law and
surrounding hills. Route-finding skills and stamina needed

8 **The Wiss from Tibbie's** 38
Two peaks reached over a mix of rough ground and old tracks,
with a lochside return to the welcoming Tibbie Shiels Inn

9 **Chasing the Grey Mare's Tail** 40
Short but steep haul by dramatic white water to climb one lofty
peak, with some exposure and extensive views

Wanlockhead's Treasures

Conrig Hill (485m), **Shiel Hill** (486m)

Walk time 8h20 Height gain 700m
Distance 28km OS Map Landranger 78

A strenuous route along good tracks and rough paths in mining territory, with a return through remote countryside. It is easy to divide this into two walks.

Start by The Museum of Lead Mining in Wanlockhead (GR872129). Walk south up Old Library Row towards the main road for 120m and turn right on a track. Pass Greenbank (a house) on its left side and start to climb a steep grassy track, which leads to old fenceposts close to the top of Black Hill. Head WNW to reach a fence on the summit plateau of Stood Hill, with great views to Glendyne Burn on descent before the steep climb to Willowgrain Hill and along the ridge on rougher ground. Soon it intersects with the Southern Upland Way. [Escape: follow the Way northeast over Glengaber Hill and back to the start, a fine walk in its own right.] Continue northwest to the summit and trig point of Conrig Hill (GR815129) (2h40). Descend north, then northeast along a vague ridge to reach a gate beside the plantation, where a track winds northwards through the forest and down to Crawick Water. Cross the bridge near the farm of Nether Cog to emerge on the main road. Walk north, cross the cattle

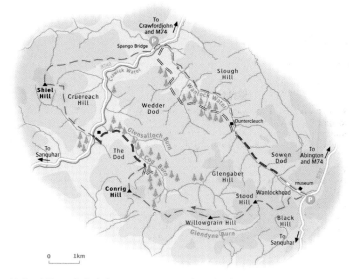

grid after 100m and climb the steep embankment to a sheep bucht, then contour round to the burn. From here, follow the fence above the water and up to the bealach on the far side of Cruereach Hill, and pass through the gate. Continue easily over Castle Hill to the summit of Shiel Hill, which gives a wide panorama of the heathery plateau to the north (GR786167) (5h). Descend NNE over clumpy ground to find a grassy track, and accompany this eastwards. Cross a fence by a gate and descend towards but keep above the fenced fields to reach a more prominent track that contours around the Dod. When you reach the road by Spango Bridge, walk northeast for 600m and turn right onto a

track marked for Wanlockhead. Cross the first of two bridges and watch for two gates on the left. Leave the track and pass through the right-hand gate to follow the Wanlock Water (popular with gold-panners) upstream. Ignore the footbridge after 600m, continuing on the east bank with rough sections but continual interest. Pass through two gates just beyond Duntercleuch, and cross a stile to join the Southern Upland Way. [Variant: from the B740, follow the main track over both bridges, up through the forest and down to Duntercleuch (longer but not so rough underfoot).] Follow the track back into the village past lead mining relics and roaming sheep (8h20).

◄ Wether Hill, Brown Hill and Willowgrain Hill from Stood Hill

Mists of Green Lowther

Green Lowther (732m)

Walk time **3h20** Height gain **400m**
Distance **9km** OS Map **Landranger 78**

Half-day walk from the historic mining village of Leadhills to climb one peak and follow a short ridge, with rough ground in both ascent and descent. Access may be restricted in grouse-shooting season.

Start by the primary school in Leadhills (GR886151). Walk south along the main road and turn left onto Horner's Place, immediately after the memorial. Follow the road in zigzags towards the golf course,

Scotland's highest, but ignore the turning to the clubhouse and continue along a track to a house 500m beyond. Pass through a gate on the left (opposite the house) to follow a grassy path to a burn. Accompany this for a short time before joining a track that takes you to the reservoir, resting quietly in the fold of the hills. Skirt around the west bank by a path to then follow the cleuch upstream on rough ground as if heading for the golf ball radar which marks the top of Lowther Hill. After 500m, when you come to an old shed, cross the water and leave the clag to climb steeply southeast by a smaller burn. This gives an entertaining journey, and

◄ Lower Hill from Black Hill

deposits you close to the humming antennae of Green Lowther (GR900120) (2h). Walk northeast and descend along the fence over Peden Head and Dungrain Law to a bealach shared with Dun Law. Leave the ridge at this point to descend northwest over heathery terrain to a burn and track. Follow this to the ruin, across Shortcleuch Water and out to the main road. Turn left and climb to the top of the pass overlooking the village. Take the track on the left which follows the line of the narrow gauge railway and swings gently round to the clubhouse. It is only a short way back to the start (3h20).

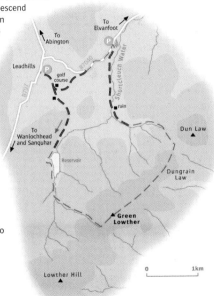

Leadhills Reading Society

Leadhills' historic library, founded by 23 miners, a schoolteacher and the minister in 1741, claims to be the oldest subscription library in Britain. Nearby Wanlockhead established its library fourteen years later making it the second oldest, although it can also claim to be the highest in the country. In the summer months, the library, with many fascinating exhibits including the walking stick of John Taylor, the miner who lived to the remarkable age of 137, is open to the public on Wednesdays and at weekends.

Steygail and Lowther Hill

Lowther Hill (725m), **Steygail** (573m),
Well Hill (606m)

Walk time 5h20 Height gain 900m
Distance 15km OS Map Landranger 78

**A strenuous walk in the Lowther Hills
with tough climbs rewarded by hidden
burns, magnificent curving ridges and
excellent views.**

Start near the top of the Dalveen Pass,
about 300m west of the county boundary
(GR910083). (There are a number of places
to park.) Go through the gate on the north
side of the road and take the path
northwest across a footbridge towards a
fence and gate. Leave the path to follow the
fence, which climbs steeply to join a blunt
spur, and then after passing a large cairn
continue over grassy slopes to the top of
Comb Head. Follow the ridge and the
county fence northwestwards over Cold
Moss and all of the way to the huge golf
ball antennae of Lowther Hill (GR890107)
(1h40). Retrace your steps for 300m, and
take the south ridge, following a grassy
track over Wether Hill. Drop to a deep
bealach below the pyramidal Steygail, and
climb this peak directly. Descend south,
then along the east ridge to Upper Dalveen:
the hill steepens just before the farm.
[Escape: cross the bridge and climb east
along a track beside the waterfalls of

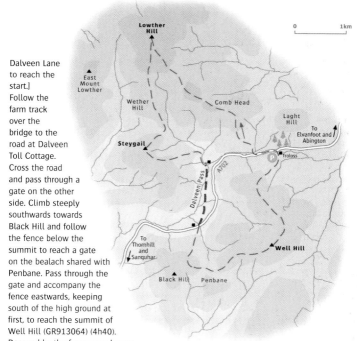

Dalveen Lane to reach the start.] Follow the farm track over the bridge to the road at Dalveen Toll Cottage. Cross the road and pass through a gate on the other side. Climb steeply southwards towards Black Hill and follow the fence below the summit to reach a gate on the bealach shared with Penbane. Pass through the gate and accompany the fence eastwards, keeping south of the high ground at first, to reach the summit of Well Hill (GR913064) (4h40). Descend by the fence over boggy ground. Pass through a gate within sight of the farm, and leave the county frontier to drop down to Troloss. A gate on the west side of the farm leads past large sheds and out to the access track, just a short way from the start (5h20).

Peden's Mist

Alexander 'Sandy' Peden was one of the most celebrated Covenanters of the 17th century and spent many years living as an outlaw, preaching at illegal conventicles in the hills across southern Scotland. As much as for his fiery preaching, he gained notoriety for his ability to evade capture. One tale has him disappearing into a mysterious mist which descended on Lowther Hill just as the Dragoons were closing in. Locally, a thick mist is still known today as Peden's Mist.

◄ Steygail from the top of the Dalveen Pass

Queensberry Rules

Queensberry (697m)

Walk time 4h20 Height gain 600m
Distance 13km OS Map Landranger 78

A rolling hill in quiet country, with some arduous climbs over boggy ground but a fine outlook across the Moffat Hills and an easy return along good tracks.

Start at the track that serves Mitchellslacks, 9km east of Thornhill (GR964960). (Parking 500m northwest or 1km south: do not block farm access.) Follow this track, cross a bridge and turn left (west) to reach the farm with a large courtyard. Rather than turn left into the

close, continue directly ahead through the metal gate where a grassy track leads you to a gate in the wall on the right after 200m. Pass through this gate and alongside the wall to another gate, which takes you out into open country. Follow the track northwards for a further 600m to reach a junction just beyond a circular sheep bucht above the Capel Burn. Take the right fork to contour around The Law, where you will see some sheep pens and a gate. Pass through the gate and ford the burn, then head southeast by a rough path, gaining gradual height to reach a small pond. Turn north from here to pass through a short rocky

◀ Ruins above Capel Burn, near Mitchellslacks

chasm before crossing or circumnavigating several rises and dips, a hard going section. Steep slopes now lead to the top of Wee Queensberry. Descend north into the quaggy flats and make the long ascent past many small cairns to the summit of Queensberry, which boasts commanding views on a good day (GR989997) (2h20). Descend northwards towards Penbreck before dropping west off the ridge. Join and follow the burn as it wanders through the solitude: you'll come to a fence just before the cottage

at Burleywhag, which leads south to a good track after 600m. Follow the track past two ruins and retrace your steps to the start (4h20).

The 39 Steps

Film buffs may spot the locations around Mitchellslacks Farm used in the 1978 film adaptation of John Buchan's thrilling spy-story *The Thirty-Nine Steps* (1915). Although there have been three different adaptations – the first by Alfred Hitchcock in 1935 – the 'Robert Powell' version stays truest to the original text. Buchan was inspired to write the story while staying with friends in North Foreland, Kent, when he heard of a German spy being captured whilst signalling from nearby cliffs.

The Devil's Beef Tub and Hart Fell

Hart Fell (808m)

Walk time 6h40 Height gain 900m
Distance 19km OS Map Landranger 78

A long ridge with many small peaks, fine views and historical interest. This route contains limited exposure, rough ground and a steep descent.

Start at the large parking area on the A701 overlooking the Devil's Beef Tub (GR055127). Walk in the direction of Tweedsmuir, watching for a path on the north side of the road just before a forestry track. Two stiles lead to open country and a short climb takes you to the top of Annanhead Hill. Follow the fence along the county boundary over Great Hill and Chalk Rig Edge: this gives a gradual increase in height to the next top, despite the many undulations. Descend steeply northeast into a hidden glen, and walk a short way south

to an old ruin below a tumbling burn. Climb east beside the burn, which falls in small cascades. Where it diminishes, continue your trajectory over the wide grassy expanse and cross the fence to reach the summit of Hart Fell (GR113136) (3h). The descent along the southeast ridge gives spectacular views into Black Hope. At the first bealach there are two gates in the fence to your right. Pass through the first of these and begin a steep southwest descent, following Auchencat Burn to give a fairly rough journey. Watch for a grassy track above the north bank of the burn, which starts about 1.5km from the bealach. This provides a much easier descent and passes under the gulch of Hartfell Spa, famous for its Merlin connections and the healing powers of its chalybeate well, before dropping slowly to reach a gate before the lower fields. Pass through this, and several

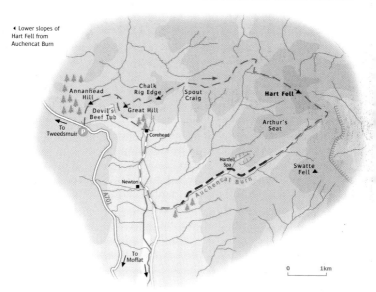

◄ Lower slopes of Hart Fell from Auchencat Burn

other gates beyond, to reach the minor road. Walk north along the road to Ericstane, cross the bridge and take the track to Corehead. Enter Corehead Old Farm (the steading at the back) and take a fenced path through the farm towards the south end of a plantation. Pass under the trees and then leave the path, climbing

diagonally northwards through the bracken to reach a gate about 250m from the trees. Pass through the gate to gain an old path above (not particularly obvious to find). This path makes for an exciting journey, with limited exposure, around the Devil's Beef Tub to the gap between Annanhead Hill and Great Hill. Return to the start (6h40).

Border reivers

The Devil's Beef Tub is a huge natural depression which earned its name for having been used by Border reivers for holding stolen cattle. From the 13th century through to the beginning of the 17th, reiving was an integral part of Border life and although livestock was the main focus of the raids, they also engaged in kidnapping and blackmail (which they invented). The lives and deeds of the reivers were celebrated in the famous *Border Ballads*, popularised by Sir Walter Scott in the 18th century.

Tweedsmuir and Talla

Mathieside Cairn (669m),
Garelet Hill (680m)

Walk time 6h20 Height gain 800m
Distance 19km
OS Maps Landranger 72 and Explorer 330

**A peaceful circuit that involves some
rough ground and very steep climbs
under Broad Law, starting by the River
Tweed and returning through forest.**

Start in Tweedsmuir (GR097244). (Limited
parking at the road junction, better at Fruid
Reservoir.) Walk northeast past the
Tweedsmuir Outdoor Centre and a row of
houses, and turn right in front of the parish
church. Cross Talla Water and pass through
a gate to join a farm track. Go through a
railway cutting, avoiding Glenrusco by
crossing a field and a footbridge beyond.
Accompany the track on its pleasant
wanderings beside the River Tweed, to
reach Hearthstane. Cross the bridge, walk
past the magnificent courtyard and turn
right, passing two large sheds, to take the
most obvious track eastwards. A gentle
walk between the forest and Hearthstane
Burn brings you to a bridge after 800m.
Continue upstream on the west bank for a
further 2km. Just before the track fords the
burn to reach an old shack and an L-shaped

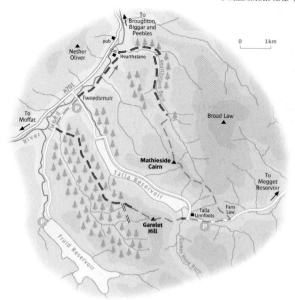

0   1km

To
Broughton,
Biggar and
Peebles

pub

Nether
Oliver

Hearthstane

Heartstone Burn

A701

Tweedsmuir

P

To
Moffat

River Tweed

Broad Law ▲

Talla Reservoir

Mathieside
Cairn ▲

To
Megget
Reservoir

Talla
Linnfoots

Fans
Law ▲

P

Garelet
Hill ▲

Games Hope Burn

Fruid Reservoir

P

forest, climb steeply west to gain the ridge at Snout Hill. Follow the old fence along this, passing Mathieside Cairn to reach the unadorned higher point beyond (GR133218) (3h). [Escape: descend westwards along a good spur to reach the road beside Talla Reservoir by a gate.] Continue along the fence as it heads ESE over rough ground, rising slightly to keep above steep cleuchs on both sides. On reaching the wide south ridge of Broad Law, drop southeast along a fence to reach the road. Walk west along the road, past a car park (alternative start point) and descend towards the reservoir. Just before the farm of Talla Linnfoots, cross

a bridge over Games Hope Burn, turn left past Witch Linn, then climb hummocky slopes to reach a gate. Pass over this and begin the tough ascent of Garelet Hill, following the water for a time before keeping closer to the arête to reach the summit (GR124202) (4h40). Accompany the fence northwest, watching for a break in the forest after about 1km. Here, cross the fence and descend west along the forest ride to reach a gravel track, the Silver Jubilee Road. Follow this northwards through the trees for 4km and down to the road by Menzion Farmhouse, leaving only a short distance back to Tweedsmuir (6h20).

◀ Garelet Hill from Tweedsmuir

35

Broad Law over Megget

Dollar Law (817m), **Broad Law** (840m)

Walk time 7h20 Height gain 1000m
Distance 22km
OS Maps Landranger 72 and 73

A full day out on some of the highest hills in the Southern Uplands, with plenty of ascent and fine views above the Megget Reservoir to reward. Good navigation skills are required.

Start at the car park at the foot of the Megget Reservoir (GR210233). Climb up to the main road and walk west for 300m. A track marked for Manor Water leads northwards along a small burn: follow this until you gain the crest of Black Rig at a large cairn on the path. Bear due west, maintaining the high ground to reach a fence that steers you first southwest and then northwest. The terrain now begins to rise towards Notman Law. Keep to the south side where there are tracks to aid progress, before continuing towards Fifescar Knowe and Dollar Law just to the north (GR178278) (2h40). Follow fences south to Dun Law and around to Cramalt Craig. Descend to a bealach and climb up the wide eastern ridge of Broad Law, where you might think you've stumbled across an extraterrestrial landing station rather than the more worldly air traffic control beacon and radio masts (GR146235) (4h20). Walk south from the top and then take the defined ridge over Porridge Cairn. Drop east towards Wylies Burn at an obvious dip before the rise to Wylies Hill, and aim for a

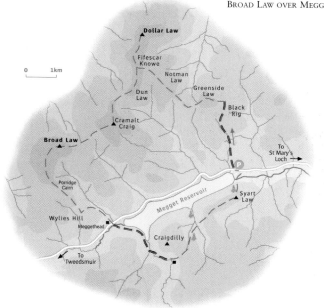

gate at the highest point of the fence. From here, tracks lead to the farm at Meggethead. Cross the road and take the gravel track above the reservoir to the farm at Winterhopeburn. A gate on the left just before the cottage gives access to the open ground above. Climb east to a bealach at Black Rig, and then follow the water north

towards Shielhope Burn. Walk between a shed and a square plantation and cross the cleuch, keeping south of the fence. Continue northeast to follow the high ground to Syart Law and its cairn on the east side. Descend to the mid point of a jaggy plantation. From here, a path leads easily to the reservoir and the start (7h20).

Edinburgh water

Megget Reservoir is Scotland's highest embankment dam and supplies the majority of Edinburgh and Lothian's water, some 100 million litres per day. Constructed in the early 1980s, it plunges to more than 50 metres at its deepest and contains 61,000 million litres of water originating from its source at Megget Water. It was built by damming a glen which held the historic ruin of Cramalt tower.

◀ Looking towards Megget Reservoir from Fans Law

The Wiss from Tibbie's

The Wiss (589m), **Peniestone Knowe** (551m)

Walk time 4h40 Height gain 600m
Distance 13km OS Map Explorer 330

A varied route which climbs two rounded peaks, with an enjoyable return by the Loch of the Lowes. Good route-finding skills are required.

Start by the café between St Mary's Loch and the Loch of the Lowes, close to the Tibbie Shiels Inn (GR237204). Cross the river between the lochs by an arched bridge and follow the Captain's Road. Continue past the inn and a radio mast to the point where the road bends to the right: a gate on the bend leads you straight along a gravel track to an intersection after 100m. Turn left to join a fence and climb alongside this until a grassy track branches off to the right after about 70m. Take this right fork to wind slowly up the hill. Where the track levels off and fades

in view of Bowerhope Forest, head ESE up hummocky grass towards The Wiss. After a short while, you can join another faint track that gives easier progress to the summit. The trig point is a short distance east on the far side of a fixed gate (1h40). Descend along the fence and then follow the edge of the vast forest southwest over boggy ground to reach a track at a cattle grid. Turn left along the track, and almost immediately take a path on the right, the waymarked Southern Upland Way. Pass through a gate to drop down through fields to Whithope Burn, a delightfully secluded spot. Cross the bridge and ascend the path past ruins and through walled fields to gain the top of Pikestone Rig. Leave the Southern Upland Way and continue over rougher ground to the summit of Peniestone Knowe, at the apex of three fences (GR236165) (3h20). Descend

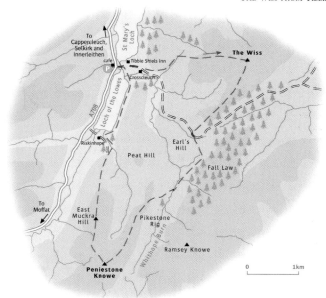

northwest along a fence and wall before following these over East Muckra Hill. Where the fence kinks left, continue due north along the apex of the ridge. Beyond a gate, head down to enclosures near Riskinhope Farm where you will reach two further gates: take the gate on the right under a large sycamore tree. Rather than drop towards the farm, walk north to a wooded burn. A track on the far side of the burn leads down to the head of the Loch of the Lowes. Follow the signposted path above the east bank of the loch to reach the old bridge and your start point (4h40).

The Tibbie

The characterful inn by St Mary's Loch takes its name from Isabella (Tibbie) Shiel who moved with her mole-catching husband Robert Richardson in 1823 into what was then known as St Mary's cottage on the estate of Lord Napier. Until her death in 1878 in her 96th year, the entertaining Tibbie played hostess to many famous literary men including the publisher Robert Chambers, James Hogg 'the Ettrick Shepherd', Sir Walter Scott, William Wordsworth, Robert Louis Stevenson and Thomas Carlyle.

Chasing the Grey Mare's Tail

White Coomb (821m)

Walk time 4h40 Height gain 700m
Distance 13km
OS Map Explorer 330 or Landranger 79

The thrills start with a climb beside what is arguably one of the finest waterfalls in Scotland, with good paths to access the main plateau and a steep descent to return through meadowland.

Start at the Grey Mare's Tail, owned by the National Trust (GR186145). Take the excellent path on the east bank of the waterfall to rise quickly above the glen, giving spectacular views of the tumbling water. Where the chasm steepens there is

some limited exposure (keep to the path), but above the two highest falls the terrain eases and gives views of the massif beyond. Continue along Tail Burn all of the way to Loch Skeen, a fine place for a picnic. Cross the burn and follow a good path that ascends a narrow ridge above the west bank of the loch to reach the top of Mid Craig and the start of the wide plateau. Traverse boggy slopes southwest, skirting around the top of Midlaw Linn, and rise gently south, crossing the fence to reach the summit of White Coomb (GR163151) (2h40). Descend southwest by the fence over wide slopes to the top of Carrifran Gans, with its gate and stile. Keep to the west side of the fenceline

◀ Nether Tarnberry and the Grey Mare's Tail

to follow the escarpment, which peers far down towards the Carrifran Burn. The ridge soon drops more abruptly, but gives no difficulty and can be followed all of the way to the road. Turn left, cross the cattle grid and climb immediately over a static gate on the right. Walk across the narrow beech plantation and pass over a similar gate by the wall on the right. Walk towards Polmoody, cross the footbridge over the Moffat Water after 200m and follow the opposite bank over two gates to reach another bridge. Cross the river again, walk just 80m on a track towards Polmoody and then turn off to continue upstream. After passing through another gate, walk through the pleasant fields between the river and the road for about 2km to reach Polmoodyburn Bridge, level with the end of the plantation to the west. Go through a gate onto the road and return to the swishing of the Grey Mare's Tail (4h40).

A hiding place

The area around White Coomb, Loch Skeen and the Grey Mare's Tail was once strongly associated with the Covenanters who sought refuge here in the 17th century, and it is likely that the name of Watch Knowe dates from the days when the hilltop was used to keep watch over the Dragoons scouring the glens below. The whole area is today in the care of the National Trust for Scotland, with a well-kept path leading from the car park up past the waterfall to Loch Skeen.

Two mighty rivers rise in the hills of the Southern Uplands. The Clyde has its origins in the Lowther and Culter hills and feeds Lanarkshire's fertile valleys on its way to becoming the celebrated main artery of the city of Glasgow. The Tweed, famed for the textile mills it once powered, begins in the Moffat Hills and journeys east through the proud Borders towns of Peebles, Galashiels and Kelso on its way to the east coast.

The first route, on Lanarkshire's popular beacon hill, Tinto, gives a wide view of the Clyde Valley. Two routes in the Culter hills follow: the first begins in the quiet village

of Lamington; the second is an adventurous hike, taking in several tops accessed from the Tweed. There is a short walk from Broughton, and a much longer horseshoe around Glensax Burn from Peebles. A route from Innerleithen tackles the forested hills above the town and returns by the river. The Yarrow Water, a tributary of the Tweed, is the venue for a meeting with the Three Brethren. Lastly, two shorter walks begin from classic Borders towns; the first makes use of the Southern Upland Way to climb a low hill above Galashiels, the other kicks off from the rugby fields of Melrose to ascend the volcanic Eildon Hills.

Clyde and Tweed

1 Adventures of Tinto   44
Short blast up an iconic hill with some rough ground and a less
usual return through woodland

2 Heatherstane Law   46
Great wildlife walk over varied and sometimes challenging terrain
to climb the peaks of Heatherstane and Whitelaw Brae

3 Gathersnow and Culter   48
Long route over Gathersnow Hill and Culter Fell, which straddle
the boundary between the Borders and South Lanarkshire

4 Trahenna and the Iron Road   50
Easier half-day circuit along the ridge above Broughton, returning
by the old Biggar railway line

5 High notes over Glensax   52
Classic circuit that starts from Peebles to climb Dun Rig,
Hundleshope Heights and several other fine peaks

6 Windlestraw over Walkerburn   54
Horseshoe of the hills north of Innerleithen, with good paths
through forestry and an enjoyable return along the River Tweed

7 Meeting with the Three Brethren   56
Amble through rolling terrain to climb Brown Knowe and the
historic Three Brethren, with fine views of the surrounding country

8 A Gala Ramble   58
Compact route that follows the Southern Upland Way before
striking out to Meigle Hill. Good route finding required

9 Roaming the Eildon Hills   60
Start from the historic Abbey to climb the popular Eildon Hills
above Melrose in this short but less conventional circuit

Adventures of Tinto

Tinto (707m)

Walk time 3h20 Height gain 500m
Distance 9km
OS Map Explorer 335 or Landranger 72

A half-day circuit of a Lanarkshire favourite that starts and finishes near the tearoom. This route contains an intricate return through the woods, and good navigation is required.

Start at the car park 300m southwest of the farm at Fallburn and the Tinto Hill tearoom (GR964374). Walk through the gate from here and follow the grassy track southwest, passing under the pylons and through a second gate to enter open country. Rather than follow the main path ahead (which is widening with use), turn left to follow the fence southeast over boggy ground until you reach a gravel track after about 400m. Follow this for a short

distance to a junction of several grassy tracks: take the one on the far left to reach a plantation wall, and follow this easily upwards. At the corner of the wall, contour under Totherin Hill to reach a minor watercourse. Keep this company until it disappears, and then clamber directly up the heathery slopes to reach the rounded ridge and the main path. Take this path to the summit of Tinto (GR952344) (2h). Step over the fence to the trig point, and walk NNW for about 400m before taking the northwest ridge. Lower down, this ridge steepens and leads to a scattering of Caledonian pine. Keep to the main line of trees that leads northwards (rather than across the slopes) to reach a gravel track by another plantation. Take the track to the road, pass through the gate and turn right. Follow the road eastwards until you are exactly 25m beyond the gravel drive that

◄ Tinto from Lamington

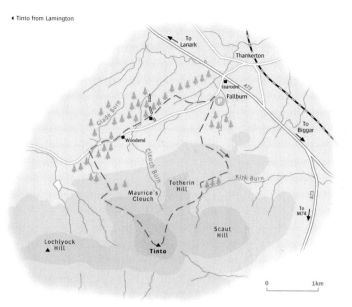

To Lanark

Thankerton

tearoom

Fallburn

P

To Biggar

Glade Burn

Woodend

Cleuch Burn

Kirk Burn

A73

Maurice's Cleuch

Totherin Hill

To M74

Lochlyock Hill ▲

Scaut Hill

Tinto

0   1km

serves Woodend. Now enter the forest on your left and find a rough track that runs parallel to the road. Continue straight on at the clearing after 100m to take a shaded path eastwards through the trees. Keeping close to the edge of the forest, cross a footbridge and follow vague trails to South

Lodge on the Carmichael Estate. Pass through the gate on the far side of the cottage and skirt along the edge of the forest. After 800m, a fence bars your way: follow it southeast, then jump the narrow burn and walk up to the gate on the road. It is just a short walk back to the start (3h20).

Carmichael Estates

Possibly Scotland's oldest single family operated farm business (since 1292) is located near Tinto hill off the A72 into Lanark. Richard Carmichael of Carmichael, 30th Chief of the Clan Carmichael, manages the estate today, which specialises in producing venison from its own herd of red deer. A farm shop and visitor centre operate on the estate, and the clan chief can also be found holding court at many farmers markets throughout Scotland.

Heatherstane Law

Heatherstane Law (Hudderstone) (626m),
Whitelaw Brae (577m)

Walk time 4h40 Height gain 500m
Distance 15km OS Map Landranger 72

**A demanding walk over several tops
with varied walking along grassy
tracks, intricate moorland paths and
rough open ground. Parts of this route
may be restricted during grouse-
shooting season.**

Start at Lamington Church (GR978309).
(There is a secluded car park between the
main road and the church.) Walk southwest
along the main road to a turning on the left
after about 100m. This junction gives three
options: take the tarmac road in the middle,
signposted for Baitlaws, and follow it for
about 700m to reach a gate on the left just
before a more ornate gateway. Pass through
the gate and take the track eastwards down
to Lamington Burn. Cross the water by a
footbridge to reach a junction shortly after:
take the track (with a gate) on the left and
climb easily towards Cowgill Loch. Follow
the fine glen, keeping an eye out for
buzzards and other interesting birds, past
the farm at Cowgill to reach the minor road.
Walk southwards: the road shortly becomes
a track which serves the two Cowgill
reservoirs. Before you reach the
embankment of the upper reservoir, leave

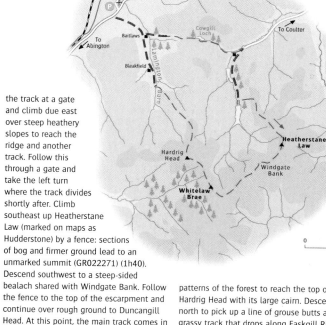

the track at a gate and climb due east over steep heathery slopes to reach the ridge and another track. Follow this through a gate and take the left turn where the track divides shortly after. Climb southeast up Heatherstane Law (marked on maps as Hudderstone) by a fence: sections of bog and firmer ground lead to an unmarked summit (GR022271) (1h40). Descend southwest to a steep-sided bealach shared with Windgate Bank. Follow the fence to the top of the escarpment and continue over rough ground to Duncangill Head. At this point, the main track comes in useful as it winds around to the summit of Whitelaw Brae (GR003260). Follow the fenceline northwest above the vast, crazy

patterns of the forest to reach the top of Hardrig Head with its large cairn. Descend north to pick up a line of grouse butts and a grassy track that drops along Easkgill Rig. Cross the burn by a bridge to reach the road at Bleakfield. A short walk along the glen takes you back to Lamington (4h40).

Divine Service in Lamington Kirk

Hopefully walkers in the area will enjoy a better day than Robert Burns did when he endured a miserable sermon in Lamington Kirk. Fond of epigrams, Burns wrote this one to a friend after the event: *As cauld a wind as ever blew, A cauld kirk, an't but few: As cauld a minister's e'er spak; Ye'se a' be het e'er I come back!*

◄ The path to Cowgill Loch from Lamington

47

Gathersnow and Culter

Gathersnow Hill (688m),
Culter Fell (748m)

Walk time 6h40 Height gain 1000m
Distance 20km OS Map Landranger 72

**Strenuous circuit over multiple peaks
with some rough ground and a river
crossing but mostly good paths.**

Start at a large layby on the A701, close
to Kingledores and by the bridge which
serves Patervan (GR107285). Head south
along the road to reach a track after 300m:
this leads west under a canopy of trees and
turns right to the steading at Kingledores.
Walk through the farm and take the track
beyond to cross Kingledoors Burn by the
bridge. From here climb north to a stand of
pine and join the path that accompanies a
small burn to the bealach between Cocklie
Rig Head and Benshaw Hill. Bear southwest
along the ridge and follow the fence on its

journey over Cocklie Rig Head and another
small knoll and then on to the top of
Glenlood Hill. Continue southwest over
Broomy Law before contouring around the
north side of Coomb Hill. Make your way as
far as the summit of Gathersnow Hill, which
gives fine views over the star-shaped
Coulter Reservoir (GR058257) (2h40).
Retrace your steps for 400m to
Glenwhappen Rig and descend north by the
fence, now marking the county boundary,
down to Holm Nick. [Escape: descend
northeast to join a path and track to
Glenkirk.] Climb north by a good path over
the flat-topped Moss Law and then over
increasingly steep slopes to the summit of
Culter Fell (GR053291) (4h20). Drop down
on the north side into boggy terrain, still
following the fence, and then climb gently
up King Bank Head. Where another fence
intersects the country boundary, head east

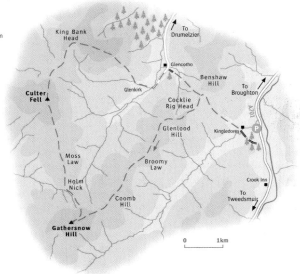

◀ Culter Fell from Snout Hill on Broad Law

along a small path which eventually leads to the top of Chapelgill Hill. Walk east for a further 300m before dropping down the southeast ridge towards Glenkirk. When approaching the farm, descend steeply to Hope Burn to reach a track down to the road. Follow the road northeast to Glencotho and, just before the house, take the track that bears southeast towards the edge of a plantation and gains height between two burns. After a while, this becomes a path and reaches the main ridge between Cocklie Rig Head and Benshaw Hill. Return from here to Kingledores and the start (6h40), perhaps stopping off at the historic Crook Inn on your way home.

Local rivals

Tradition has it that Culter Fell and Tinto, a few miles to the north, are almost the same altitude, an old couplet suggesting that 'Between Tintock tap and Culter Fell, but scarce three handbreadths and an ell' (an ell being the old Scots measure of roughly 37 inches). In fact, Culter Fell is 41 metres higher, which may explain why local walkers have been carrying stones to the top of Tinto for generations in order to add stature to the substantial cairn at the summit.

Trahenna and the Iron Road

Trahenna Hill (549m)

Walk time 3h40 Height gain 350m
Distance 11km OS Map Landranger 72

A half-day route mostly on good paths and tracks with easy navigation and great views along the upper Tweed.

Start in the village of Broughton (GR112365). Walk 170m north of the intersection with the B7016 (to Biggar) to a road on the right, with a footpath sign marked for Stobo. Follow this road and the John Buchan Way uphill, bypass the first farm on its left side and walk beyond Broughton Place to a solitary house (walkers' car park here, with limited spaces). Pass through a gate and continue along a

track that rises above a small plantation and crosses Hollows Burn. About 1km further on, the track comes to a large open corrie between the three peaks of Clover Law, Broomy Side and Hammer Head. Climb eastwards to join the bealach between the latter two peaks, where a fence leads southeast along the ridgeline to the top of Hammer Head. Bear south along the pleasantly undulating ridge to Trahenna Hill: a meeting of three walls on the plateau gives the best access eastwards to its summit (GR135374) (2h20). Descend due south along the ridge and, when drawing close to the farm at Dreva, cut southeast into the glen to arrive at the farm buildings. Walk westwards along the road to a

◀ The copse above Llolans, on the outskirts of Broughton

junction, and take the lower road towards Rachan. About 100m beyond Dreva Cottage, a gate offers access down towards a bend in the River Tweed. The old railway to Biggar and beyond, once the route of the Tinto Express, lies between the road and the river, and this can be followed all of the way to Broughton. Its rails have been removed but it provides an excellent track with cuttings, embankments and a bridge. On approaching the first houses in Broughton, cross the burn by a small footbridge, and follow the minor road into the village (3h40).

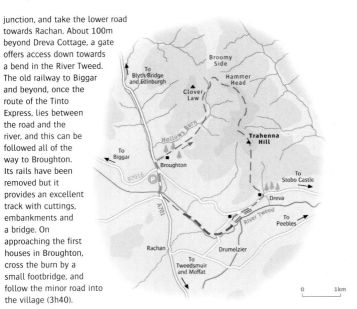

Baron Tweedsmuir

The author and diplomat John Buchan (1875-1940), whose varied career included the roles of editor of *The Spectator*, Director of Information during World War I and Governor-General of Canada, was born in Perth but later moved with his family to the Borders. Best known as author of the popular spy thriller *The Thirty-Nine Steps*, he also wrote more serious works such as *Witch Wood* (1927), set in the Borders during the religious struggles of the 17th century, which more fully display his talents. The John Buchan Centre in Broughton can provide details of the John Buchan Way which covers some 22km (13 miles), from Peebles to Broughton, taking in part of Cademuir Hill and passing close to Barns Tower, the settings for two of his lesser-known stories.

51

High notes over Glensax

Dun Rig (744m),
Hundleshope Heights (685m)

Walk time 7h Height gain 750m
Distance 21km OS Map Landranger 73

**A rollercoaster of a route south of
Peebles with good paths to start,
leading to rougher ground and a series
of short, exhilarating climbs.**

Start at the southeast end of Glen Road
View in Kings Muir, 1km from the centre of
Peebles (GR260392). Walk southeast
through the trees along a prominent track
and footpath marked for Yarrow. Cross
Glensax Burn and begin a steady climb,

which shortly brings you onto the open fell.
The first hill can be climbed or turned on
the north side, leading to a small dip and a
gate. Beyond the gate, follow the path
sandwiched between two dry-stone dykes
to walk over the top of Kailzie Hill and
Kirkhope Law. Continue along the edge of
the Cardrona Forest and up to the summit
of Birkscairn Hill. Shadow the fence down to
a bealach and continue over Stake Law
(here, progress is hard across the ruptured
bog), before the gentle climb to the top of
Dun Rig (GR254316) (4h). Continue
southwest, following the fenceline until it
makes more sense to contour around to join

the north spur of the hill. This makes it easy to drop down to Glenrath Heights. Climb northwards over the undulating plateau that constitutes Middle Hill and Broom Hill, before descending gently to the trig point at Hundleshope Heights (GR250339). Follow the posts or head due north towards Preston Law. Descend steeply from here and rise to the obvious pap of Newby Kipps, whose summit is marked by the convergence of three dykes. Follow the wall northwest to descend to an area of flat ground and a gate. Go through the gate, and head north into the forest by a track. This divides after 400m: take the right fork to gain some height before dropping and winding your way down into farmland. Cross a field by gates to reach a road, which passes the grand villas of Haystoun and leads directly back to the start (7h).

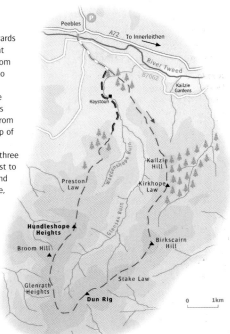

Ospreys over the Tweed

Being a rare species, the eggs and skins of ospreys were highly prized by Victorian collectors, and by the early 20th century the bird was almost extinct in Scotland. Thanks to the efforts of several conservation bodies, however, the Scottish population of ospreys is now thriving and a breeding pair have recently nested in the Tweed Valley Forest Park. Webcam images of their eyrie can be viewed in the summer months at Glentress Forest and Kailzie Gardens Visitor Centres.

◀ Peebles skyline

Windlestraw over Walkerburn

Windlestraw Law (south summit) (657m)

Walk time 6h Height gain 500m
Distance 19km OS Map Landranger 73

An undulating ridge reached mostly on good paths, though with some boggy sections and a riverside return.

Start at the centre of Innerleithen (GR333367). Walk east through the town, cross the bridge over the Leithen Water and take the second turn on the left after 100m, a small lane marked as Horsburgh Terrace. At the end of the lane, a path heads up through the trees: follow this to a junction and take the right fork (marked with blue arrows) to a panorama point with a circle of seven carvings. Descend steeply, cross another path and take the path ahead: this rises along the edge of the ridge to Pirn Craig with forest on the left and open

fell/clear cut to the right. When you reach a track, cross straight over to climb through forest towards Kirnie Law. A path skirts this hill on its south side before dropping north to the large concrete shell that has become a canvas for local artists. Continue north over Priesthope Hill and descend steeply, keeping a large plantation on the left. Rise up to Glede Knowe, and cross to the right side of the low north-south fence if you haven't done so already. Walk ENE over boggier ground, following a different fence to the southern summit of Windlestraw Law: a cairn on the other side of the fence marks the top (GR362420) (3h). [Detour: the north summit is slightly higher but lies 1.5km away over rough ground (add 40 min).] Head south, where a fence and wall can be followed over increasingly solid ground. Walk easily over Scawd Law and

◀ The Tweed Valley from Walker Burn

down to a gate. Pass though the gate, ignoring the track that drops eastwards, and climb Cairn Hill, which is wedged between plantations. From the top, descend by a small path along the forest rise, passing a second cairn, to reach a clearing and a grassy track. Turn right to follow the track northwest as it traverses the hillside and drops in a hairpin by the Walker Burn to the ruin of Priesthope. Take the track that leads southwards through the trees to open ground and on through three gates and past farm buildings to reach the A72 in Walkerburn. Cross the road and take the minor road directly opposite for 60m. Now take the lane between the industrial area and the school: this soon becomes a pleasant grassy track that crosses fields before hugging the north bank of the River Tweed. After about 2km, walk under the old railway bridge and immediately pass through a gate on the right. This leads to a path which runs behind the caravan park. Follow the path back to the centre of Innerleithen (6h).

Printing in Innerleithen

Robert Smail's Printing Works on Innerleithen High Street is a completely restored printing works with composing and press rooms where visitors can watch a traditional letterpress printer at work. Until 1986, when the National Trust for Scotland took over, the Smail family printed almost everything in the local community including a weekly newspaper from 1893 to 1916. The very first press in Scotland was set up by Walter Chepman and Androw Myllar of Edinburgh in 1508, fifty years after the Gutenberg Bible was published in Germany.

Meeting with the Three Brethren

Three Brethren (464m),
Brown Knowe (523m)

Walk time 4h Height gain 500m
Distance 12km OS Map Landranger 73

**An easy half-day route which follows a
ridge on the Southern Upland Way and
returns on good tracks to a youth hostel
with a place in history.**

Start by the public telephone in
Yarrowford (GR408300). (Parking in the
village.) Walk east along the main road to
the bridge over the River Yarrow. Turn left
here and follow the minor road north for
70m. Take a narrow path on the right, in
front of a turreted house: this makes for a
delightful journey through rhododendrons
and above a steep, wooded gorge to the
Broadmeadows Youth Hostel. Take the path
on the right hand side of the hostel and
continue above the burn to reach a wall at
the end of the trees. After passing through a
gate in the wall, turn right and go through a
second gate to gain a grassy track. Turn
right again, and walk south for about 50m
to reach a wide gravel track on the left.
Follow this eastwards as it snakes uphill
and over the ridge of Foulshiels Hill.
Descend into a wide bowl where the track
becomes grassy and leads to a gate. Beyond

the gate, continue to drop gently to reach an intersection of paths after 200m. Turn left, climbing north through heather to gain the unmistakable summit of the Three Brethren: its cairns marking the boundary between three estates (GR433319) (1h40). Walk westwards along the Southern Upland Way. [Escape: after 1.5km, a marked path descends south to the youth hostel.] Pass north of Broomy Law and south of the next top beside a line of wind-bent old pine.

A final climb takes you to the top of Brown Knowe. Cross the stile to the cairn, and descend the hummocky south ridge by a wall and fence. Where the terrain levels and the fence scissors the wall, drop west over heather to reach a fine grassy path, the Minchmoor Road. This leads along the ridge and widens lower down in the shadow of a forest. Pass through several gates to meet a gravel track which leads easily down into Yarrowford and back to the start (4h).

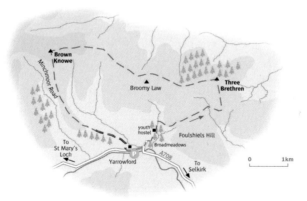

Youth Hostels

The world's first youth hostel was opened on 29 August 1909 by Richard Schirrmann, a German schoolteacher who was concerned that children in the industrial cities had no experience of the countryside. He later founded the German Youth Hostel Association, but was forced to resign by the Nazis in 1936. The first hostel operated by the Scottish Youth Hostel Association opened at Broadmeadows in 1931, and today the organisation provides about 4500 (usually very comfortable) beds in over 70 hostels.

◄ Woodland above Broadmeadows by Yarrowford

A Gala Ramble

Meigle Hill (423m)

Walk time 3h Height gain 300m
Distance 9km OS Map Landranger 73

A small but interesting hill reached by good paths from an historic Border town. This walk contains some tricky route finding through forestry and across farmland.

Start at the War Memorial in the centre of Galashiels (GR490360). Walk west along St John Street and enter Scott Park. Cross the park to its northern side, keeping north of the school to pick up the thistle signs marking the Southern Upland Way.

A footbridge marks your exit from the park out to a minor road, where you now take a path into woodland. The signs are easy to follow, indicating left at the next two junctions to lead you southwards through the trees to green fields. Head for the far left corner of the first field and straight up the brow of the hill. Continue through the trees and across open ground again. Pass over a stile just after the highest point and,

instead of continuing along the Southern Upland Way, bear westwards for 200m, passing giant rock heaps to reach a gate in the wall. Beyond the gate, grassy tracks lead northwest towards Neidpath Hill. Two further gates bring you out on the ridge, with views across a heathery bowl and down to the River Tweed. It is not possible to cross the wall that snakes along Mossilee Hill: instead descend slightly into the bowl to pass through a small gate about 100m south of the summit plantation. Climb through the field beyond to a gate, which gives access to a concrete track. Take this to reach the three antennae and Wallace's Putting Stone on the summit of Meigle Hill (GR466360) (2h20). Descend easily northeast by a grassy path that runs parallel to the forest to reach a fenced structure and the end of a track. Take this for 100m and enter the field on the right, dropping down to reach Manse Lane by a gate near the farm sheds. Descend to Gala Park and back to the centre of town (3h).

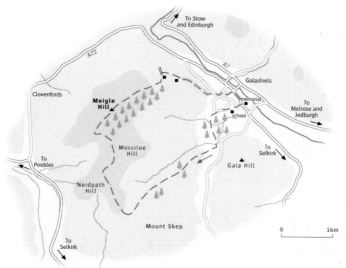

◀ Lambs and Gala Hill, above Galashiels

Roaming the Eildon Hills

Eildon Hills (422m)

Walk time 3h20 Height gain 300m
Distance 9km
OS Map Landranger 73 or Explorer 338

Half-day circuit of the Eildon Hills with an intricate approach through dense wood and farmland.

Start at Melrose Abbey (GR548341). Walk west along Buccleuch Street and turn right to walk past Melrose RFC. Climb to the junction at the top of the hill and take the left turn for Darnick. Turn left onto Chiefswood Road after 600m, pass under the A6091 and take the first turn on the right into the hospital grounds. Follow the winding access road WNW towards the Wooden Spoon Centre of Achievement (rather than going towards the hospital) to reach a minor road on the west. Turn left along the road, bearing right at the Carecentre and Achnacree. Take the next left onto a track to pass Rhymer's Cottage. When the track begins to wind uphill and you are level with a large pylon in the middle of a field, watch for a grassy track on the right. Take this into the forest: after a clearing it becomes a path and enters deep forest with occasional boggy sections. Higher up, the path curves delightfully through the trees, shadowing a hidden burn. Escape the dark canopy and pass through a gate in the wall to reach rough open ground. An awkward southwards climb takes you to a gate in the fence at the top of the ridge. Pass through this and walk east, parallel to the Bowden Moor plantation. Go through two more gates to

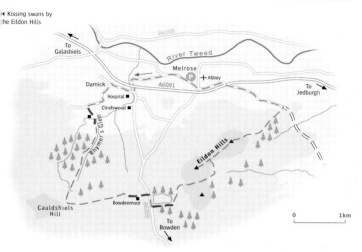

◄ Kissing swans by the Eildon Hills

reach a gravel track, then turn right to pass through Bowdenmoor Farm and out to the road. Turn right and walk 200m south, just beyond a lochan and a wood. A gate on the left leads you along a track and through another gate to the hillside. Climb northeast over grassy slopes towards the Eildon Hills. After passing through a gate, you reach a path that twists through the heather before joining St Cuthbert's Way which takes you up to the col between the two principal summits. [Escape: descend north along St Cuthbert's Way to Melrose.] [Detour: climb the higher Mid Hill along obvious paths, before returning to the col.] Follow a wide grassy path northeast to North Hill (GR554328) (2h40). Descend northeast by another good path that leads directly to a minor road that serves Stone. Walk westwards along the road towards historic Melrose and the Abbey (3h20).

The Romans

Unlike England, Scotland never became part of the Roman Empire, although it was not for the want of trying. Several incursions were made into southern Scotland from 80AD on and for periods of time local tribes made treaties with the Romans allowing them to establish several important strongholds including Trimontium, 3km east of Melrose. The hill fort on Eildon's north hill acted as a signalling position during this period, but was re-occupied by local tribes when the Romans withdrew behind Hadrian's Wall in 118AD.

Close to the capital city of Edinburgh, three ranges of hills rise up: the Lammermuirs, heathery and striped; the Moorfoots, blinking with wind turbines; and the Pentlands, ever popular with the city's walkers, cyclists and runners.

The high relief of the Southern Uplands precipitates warm air masses flowing from the Atlantic, leaving the coastal plain of the Lothians basking in the rain shadow of the mountains. The plain is not quite flat, though, and boasts many small hills that jot a disjointed line from west to east. This land once seethed with tectonic movement to create some wild formations, including Bass Rock and the site of Edinburgh Castle.

The first excursion climbs the old volcano of Arthur's Seat. Three routes explore the Pentlands: one over Scald Law from Balerno; a second from Flotterstone encompasses most of the Pentland skyline; and a third makes a rough circuit from West Linton. Two circuits venture into the Moorfoot Hills: a leisurely climb from Eddleston and some wild walking from Gladhouse Reservoir. The final two treks span the Lammermuir Hills: a river stroll from Longformacus and a circuit of Whiteadder Reservoir.

Edinburgh and Lothian

1 **King of Edinburgh** 64
Journey through the heart of Edinburgh to explore Arthur's Seat, with plenty of geological and cultural interest along the way

2 **The Pentlands' Sunday Best** 66
Gentle walk over two Pentland hills, starting near a nature reserve and passing through the picturesque Green Cleuch

3 **Flotterstone and the Pentland Rising** 68
Fine route that traverses much of the Pentland skyline, with an intricate return by woodland and an ancient hill fort

4 **To the Cauldstane Slap** 70
Pleasant approach from West Linton to ascend rugged moorland tops with some stunning views

5 **The Dundreich Ring** 72
Intricate walk across farmland to climb one fine peak, returning by a reservoir and an ancient hill fort to Eddleston

6 **Blackhope Scar from Gladhouse** 74
A ravine and a ruined castle add to the entertainment on this long and sometimes arduous route in the Moorfoot Hills

7 **All Along the Watch Water** 76
Heathery walk with a riverside start, some rough terrain and a gentle return along the Southern Upland Way

8 **Spartleton Edge over Whiteadder** 78
Half-day adventure in the Lammermuir Hills, taking in a reservoir, a forgotten castle and a rounded peak

King of Edinburgh

Arthur's Seat (251m)

Walk time 3h20 Height gain 300m
Distance 10km OS Map Explorer 350

An undemanding circuit of Edinburgh's own mountain that starts with a short bus journey and returns through the historic Old Town.

Start by the National Gallery on the Mound just off Princes Street (GR255737). Cross the road to catch an eastbound bus (numbers 26, 44 and others) towards Meadowbank and Portobello. Ride about a dozen stops to alight in front of Meadowbank Stadium (20 min). Walk east to the first traffic lights and cross London Road. Turn right onto Meadowbank Terrace and continue straight on at the mini-roundabout to St Margaret's Loch, popular with swans, Canada Geese and children alike. Walk along the far bank before turning left to climb steeply up to the ruins of St Anthony's Chapel. Head towards the hulk of the mountain and begin a gradual ascent along the Dry Dam. Where the path forks, trend left by a grassy path that leads under the amphitheatre to reach a small bealach above Dunsapie Loch. Climb steeply south to reach a chain fence and take the rocky path to the summit of Arthur's Seat, with commanding views of the City of Edinburgh and the Firth of Forth (GR275729) (1h20). From the rocky outcrop that supports the trig point, return to the

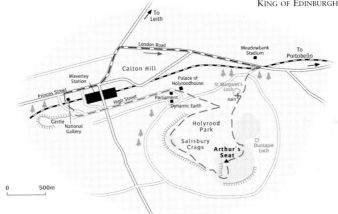

start of the chains and almost double back by a smooth grassy incline on the right (this avoids a step descent south from the top). Walk south over a grassy bump (The Lion's Haunch) and contour northwest to reach a junction of paths. Descend the steps to the right, which lead in zigzags beside the gully to the head of a broad glen. [Escape: walk north into Hunter's Bog and the lower park.] Climb north along the sharp profile of Salisbury Crags to the top of Cat Nick: the sheer dolerite edge gives uninterrupted views over the contrasting architecture of Holyrood Palace, the Scottish Parliament and Dynamic Earth.

Continue along the escarpment and descend to the road to pass clockwise around the Palace to the front of the Parliament buildings. Start the long walk up the Royal Mile towards the Castle. (This road begins as the Canongate and becomes the High Street and then the Lawnmarket as it approaches the Castle.) Pass St Giles' Cathedral and cross the busy junction of the Lawnmarket by the David Hume Statue. Watch for Lady Stair's Close on the right, 50m after the junction, home to the fascinating Writers' Museum. Descend the steps beyond to leave a short walk down to the galleries (3h20).

The Scottish Parliament

From the top of Arthur's Seat, looking down on Edinburgh, you will see the embodiment of Scotland's political and cultural will, the Scottish Parliament. Designed by Catalan architect Enric Miralles, who died in 2000, before its completion, it was inspired by upturned fishing boats and the paintings of Charles Rennie Mackintosh. It is, in Miralles words, an 'extended conversation' between the city and its citizens, and not 'a building in a park or garden, but of the land'.

◀ Edinburgh and Salisbury Crags

The Pentlands' Sunday Best

West Kip (550m), **Scald Law** (579m)

Walk time 4h40 Height gain 400m
Distance 15km
OS Map Explorer 344 or Landranger 66

A Pentland walk along reservoirs and past a waterfall, with no difficulties and good paths and tracks throughout. The start of this route is easily accessible by bus from Edinburgh.

Start at the Harlaw House Ranger Centre and wildlife garden (GR181653). (Good parking and only a short distance from the bus terminus at Balerno.) Take the Harlaw Forest Walk, which leads clockwise around Harlaw Reservoir through Scots pine to the embankment of Threipmuir Reservoir. Walk west along the top of the dam, cross the outflow and join a track between trees and fields. After a short diversion by a shed, continue for 300m to a bend in the track. Now follow the signs for Nine Mile Burn through slender birch to reach a tarmac road. Turn left, pass the Red Moss of Balerno, one of the few remaining raised peat bogs in the Lothians, and walk up the grand beech-lined avenue to a T-junction. Turn right here and left after about 60m to

pass over a stile into open country. A grassy track leads through a gate/stile and across moorland to meet the ridge. Rather than continue on the track to Nine Mile Burn, climb east by a path to the airy summit of West Kip. Drop steeply east, walk over East Kip and take a slanting path on the north side of the ridge to gain the summit and trig point of Scald Law (GR192611) (3h). Descend northeast to a prominent bealach shared with Carnethy Hill. Cross the fence and descend northwest by a gravel track, the Old Kirk Road, to reach The Howe, at the head of Loganlea Reservoir. Walk upstream, past a romantic waterfall and through the lovely Green Cleuch, to find a path on the right just before a stile. This climbs a short way before dropping gently beside a wall under the western flanks of Black Hill. When you reach a sandstone hut, cross the narrow isthmus across Threipmuir Reservoir. Turn right immediately beyond and, after 100m,

pass through a stile on the left. Follow a path through young trees and over several stiles to the shade by Harlaw Reservoir, just a short distance from the start (4h40).

Robert Louis Stevenson

The Old Kirk Road over the Pentlands to Glencorse Church in Penicuik was a scenic route to Sunday worship for many Edinburgh folk, including the celebrated writer Robert Louis Stevenson. Between 1867 and 1880, his parents regularly rented a cottage in the summer months at Swanston and the views of the city he gained walking in the surrounding hills inspired his early work *Edinburgh: Picturesque Notes* (1879).

◀ The northern Pentlands from Harlaw Reservoir

Flotterstone and the Pentland Rising

Carnethy Hill (573m), **Black Hill** (501m),
Allermuir Hill (493m)

Walk time 6h20 Height gain 1000m
Distance 19km
OS Map Explorer 344 or Landranger 66

**A rollercoaster of many small peaks
with good paths to access. For more
frequent Edinburgh bus services, use
the alternative start point near the ski
centre at Hillend.**

Start at the Pentland Hills Regional Park
Ranger Centre at Flotterstone (GR233631).
Follow the Glen Road towards Glencorse
Reservoir, turning left onto the footpath
(signposted for Scald Law) after about
400m. Cross the burn after a further 100m
and climb the grassy embankment. Go over

a stile and start the steep ascent past a
clump of weathered pine and onto the
shoulder of Turnhouse Hill. Walk over the
top and down to a bealach before the sharp
climb to the summit of Carnethy Hill
(GR204619) (2h). Descend westwards along
the main ridge to a bealach shared with
Scald Law. Cross the fence and drop
diagonally northwest down the slopes to
reach the enchanting Green Cleuch close to
The Howe. Turn right, cross Logan Burn and
walk east along the private road for 400m
to find a grassy track on the left
immediately before a bridge. [Escape:
continue along the road to Flotterstone.]
Follow the track in a wide arc to the
summit of Black Hill, then drop northeast to
the boggy gap shared with Bell's Hill. Keep
to the fence on the north side of the slopes
to reach an east-west path below Harbour
Hill. After climbing this knoll, drop north

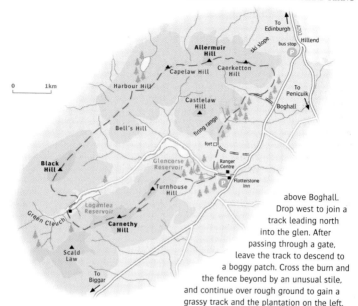

and then, steering clear of the plantation, walk steeply up Capelaw Hill. Descend northeast, cross a stile and a track, and ascend Allermuir Hill (with trig point) (GR227662) (4h40). Walk east to climb to the craggy double summit of Caerketton Hill. From the east top, descend steeply northeast. Cross the stile and turn right, following signs for Boghall down to the edge of a plantation. [Variant: an alternative approach to this route is from Hillend. Follow signs for Boghall from the entrance to the ski slopes.] Go over a stile, skirt along the edge of the plantation and cross another stile to reach three wooden masts above Boghall. Drop west to join a track leading north into the glen. After passing through a gate, leave the track to descend to a boggy patch. Cross the burn and the fence beyond by an unusual stile, and continue over rough ground to gain a grassy track and the plantation on the left. Contour around Woodhouselee Hill beside old pine. Drop into the bowl, where there are rough tracks, and then keep to the line of trees to gain the southeast ridge of Castlelaw Hill. Follow the dry watercourse to join a track by the firing range, which takes you down to Castlelaw Fort, an Iron Age hill fort with an underground chamber. Walk through the car park, where a path bypasses Castlelaw Farm on the south side to join a track. Follow the track for 200m and take the signposted path on the left for Flotterstone: this leads directly down to the private road, leaving only a short distance back to the start (6h20).

◄ Glencorse Reservoir and Turnhouse Hill

To the Cauldstane Slap

West Cairn Hill (562m),
Mount Maw (535m)

Walk time 6h20 Height gain 600m
Distance 21km OS Map Landranger 72

**A circle of several peaks around the
Baddinsgill Reservoir, starting from a
conservation village and covering some
very rough ground.**

Start at St Andrew's Parish Church in
West Linton (GR149515). Walk north along
Main Street to the Gordon Arms Hotel on
the A702, and cross it to follow the gravel
road that begins directly opposite the pub.
After 2km, take the second sharp left turn
to descend to Stonypath. Bypass the farm
on its north side and continue along a
grassy track around the shoulder of Faw
Mount. Where the track drops towards

Baddinsgill House, take the signposted path
down to Lyne Water. Follow this upstream
for a short distance, cross the water by the
footbridge and climb up to the road. Walk
north, cross a cattle grid and, after 70m,
take the path into the woods on the left.
This soon leaves the woodland by a gate,
where a grassy track leads alongside a
plantation to another gate. Go through this
to accompany a fence westwards to the top
of Byrehope Mount. Descend northwest
over increasingly rough terrain to a complex
bealach between three peaks. Cross an old
fence to start climbing north near Wolf
Craigs, and pass over a fixed gate. Easier
ground leads up a defined ridge, baring
occasional hints of the underlying
sandstone. The summit of West Cairn Hill
lies at the far end of the ridge, crowned

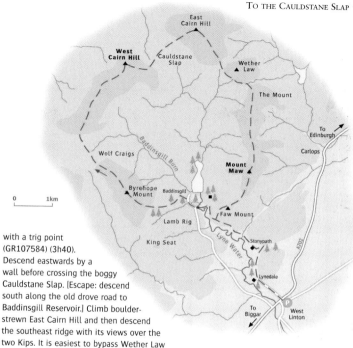

with a trig point
(GR107584) (3h40).
Descend eastwards by a
wall before crossing the boggy
Cauldstane Slap. [Escape: descend
south along the old drove road to
Baddinsgill Reservoir.] Climb boulder-
strewn East Cairn Hill and then descend
the southeast ridge with its views over the
two Kips. It is easiest to bypass Wether Law
on its south side before the short climb to
The Mount. From here, follow the wide
ridge over a couple of knolls to the summit
of Mount Maw (GR141555) (5h20). Descend

the south ridge, keeping close to the wall,
then circumvent Faw Mount on its west
side to reach the original grassy track.
Retrace your steps to the start (6h20).

Drove Road

The Cauldstane Slap, the pass between East and West Cairn Hills, was the highest point on
the drove road used for moving sheep and cattle between Falkirk and Peebles. West Linton
was also home to one of the largest sheep fairs in Scotland and tolls were collected at the
town's tollhouse from drovers bringing their livestock through. On the other side of the
hills, Cairns Castle is the ancestral home of the family which, through an Irish-born
governor, gave its name to the city of Cairns in Australia.

◀ The Kips from East Cairn Hill

71

The Dundreich Ring

Dundreich (622m)

Walk time 4h Height gain 500m
Distance 12km OS Map Landranger 73

**Good route-finding skills are required
for this route which climbs Dundreich
above Eddleston by good paths and
tracks, returning through woodland.**

Start at the Horseshoe Inn in Eddleston
(GR243472). Walk eastwards up Bellfield
Road to a junction by the parish church.
Leave the road to carry straight on both
here and at the next junction, continuing
along the grassy lane to a gate beneath
Scots pine (200m). Pass through the gate

and climb beside the wall towards the line
of beech. Go through the gate in the (east)
corner of the field and immediately through
another on your left to enter the wood,
where a grassy track leads you southeast to
a gate. Cross diagonally left over the
sloping field beyond, aiming for a gap
between two walled plantations after 300m.
Pass through a wooden gate and, keeping
the trees on your left, descend to a dip.
Now the real climbing begins, first beside
old pine (through another gate) and then
close to a wall that runs the length of Milky
Law. A prominent track intersects where the
ground levels: climb east to follow this and

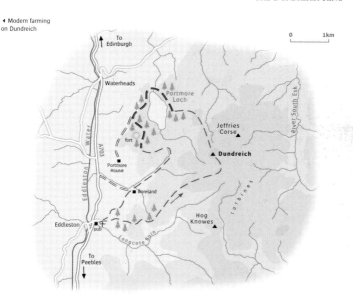

◀ Modern farming
on Dundreich

the thwacking of the wind turbines ahead. Leave the track when it fades and rise north over heathery slopes to gain the plateau. Climb over the gate on the south top to make the short way to the summit of Dundreich (GR273491) (2h). Lose height quickly by following the wall NNW to the corner of a plantation: pass through the gate on the right and continue in the shadow of the evergreens to the quiet shores of Portmore Loch. Walk north around the reservoir, crossing the dam to continue by another track on the opposite bank and through the woods, turning left after 600m. This leads steadily upwards

(ignore the next turn on the left) to reach Northshield Rings, the subtle remains of an ancient hill fort. Take the right branch by the heathery circles and drop easily through the Portmore estate to a gateway after 300m. Turn left just before the fence to follow a faint grassy track over the top of the hill, doubling back slightly to reach a gate by upright pine. Walk through the gate and over a mound to meet a main track. Follow this southwest along the glen to Boreland and a junction just beyond the farm. Walk through the gate directly ahead to reach the original beech wood. Retrace your steps to the start (4h).

73

Blackhope Scar from Gladhouse

Blackhope Scar (651m)

Walk time 6h Height gain 400m
Distance 20km OS Map Landranger 73

**A long traverse that starts along a
reservoir and follows the River South
Esk, with rough ground over the tops
contrasting with the easier paths and
tracks in approach and return. Dogs
cannot be taken on this route.**

Start at the junction of minor roads at the
northeast end of Gladhouse Reservoir
(GR304543). (Parking areas on the north and
east sides of the reservoir.) Walk south
along the single-track road to a T-junction.
Turn right along the farm track to Mauldslie,
but leave this after 30m and pass through a
gate on the left side of the farm. A
signposted path leads through the middle
of a field to the corner of a plantation,
where the path now takes you through a
second field to a cattle grid and a junction
of tracks. Follow the gravel track on the
right to the smart Huntly Cottages and
continue to Moorfoot. Just after a sharp
bend and a barn on the left, turn left
towards a row of cottages. Bypass this row
by the track on the right to head
southwards past the ruins of Hirendean
Castle and along the River South Esk.
Where the track starts to climb west (by a
cottage) after 3km, continue upstream
instead. At the first major confluence in the

river (about 1km beyond the cottage), ascend by the right hand tributary known as the Long Cleave. A last haul brings you out onto the summit and trig point of Blackhope Scar, with views of the wind turbines of the nearby hills (GR315483) (3h20). Follow the county fence in a wide northerly arc over the boggy terrain of The Kipps and all of the way to Mauldslie Hill: this is fairly tough going, especially when wet. Descend to a bealach shared with Torfichen Hill and pass through the gate to the north side of the fence. Drop westwards along an old path, which then takes you over the lush grass south of two diamond-shaped plantations. Turn north after the second clump of trees to reach a gate, and follow the old watercourse beyond. Cut across a field to reach the road at a gate, close to Mauldslie. Retrace your steps to the start (6h).

Pink-footed Geese

Recognised as a Site of Special Scientific Interest, Gladhouse in the Moorfoot Hills attracts some of the 50,000 or so Pink-footed Geese which make their way from their breeding grounds in Iceland and Greenland in September and October every year to roost at various sites around Scotland. Other recent rare birds sited here when the water levels drop to attract mud-waders have included American Wigeon, Ring-billed Gull and White-winged Black Tern.

◄ Dundreich from Mauldslie

All Along the Watch Water

Twin Law (447m)

Walk time 5h40 Height gain 300m
Distance 21km OS Map Landranger 67

A long approach from Longformacus to climb two hills on a mix of paths and rough ground. In grouse-shooting season, some sections of this route may not be accessible.

Start at the bend in the road in Longformacus, 100m northwest of the bridge (GR691573). Walk westwards along the winding gravel track, signposted to Horseupcleuch via Dye Water. Just before Glebe Cottage, after about 700m, turn right to skirt along the edge of a forest and pass through a gate to enter open country. A vague grassy path leads west and is easier to shadow as Dye Water comes into view. After passing a corrugated iron shed, follow the fence and then go through a gate on your right to enter a field: this gives easier walking. The path, though occasionally hard to trace, continues with interest, passing through various gates and crossing minor burns to eventually reach a track close to Dye Cottage. Walk to the buildings and cross the river by the bridge. Head south up the gravel track, passing grouse butts to reach a cairn marked JOH 1994. [Escape: Continue south along the track to Watch Water and follow the Southern Upland Way to the start.] Just beyond the cairn on the

◀ The windswept Watch Water

right, a path leads west over gentle slopes to the top of Dunside Hill. Drop southwest over difficult terrain to the upper reaches of Watch Water and then climb to a gate in a wall, west of the summit of Twin Law. Go through the gate and continue to the monumental cairns which mark the summit (GR624548) (3h20). Descend easily east along the wide path of the Southern Upland Way. On reaching a track, turn left and ford Watch Water. Turn right at the next junction to reach the farm at Scarlaw. Walk along the road above the reservoir to the

large building next to the dam. Just beyond the building, a gate on the left leads to a field overlooking the outlet burn. Traverse this field, where an old grassy track then takes you through two more gates and down to the burn. Cross the metal footbridge and the stile beyond to enter a large field, which should be climbed south to reach the farm at Rawburn. [Variant: in spate, it is preferable to follow the road from the reservoir.] Walk eastwards along the road back to Longformacus (5h40).

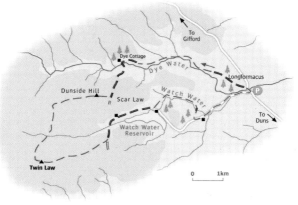

Southern Upland Way

Lowther Hill marks the highest point on the Southern Upland Way, a waymarked coast-to-coast footpath which covers 340km (212 miles) from Portpatrick in the west to Cockburnspath in the east. Opened in 1984, the route is tackled by around 1000 long-distance walkers a year, taking anything from nine and twenty days to complete.

Spartleton Edge over Whiteadder

Spartleton (468m)

Walk time 3h20 Height gain 350m
Distance 9km OS Map Landranger 67

A short but intricate circuit with many old tracks, occasional bog and plenty of interest for water lovers.

Start at the east end of Whiteadder Reservoir on the B6355, by a parking area and picnic tables (GR666633). Head for the house on the north side of the road, where a gravel track on the right hand side of the house zigzags north to reach a gate after 200m. Pass through the gate and, rather than follow the main track east, take a grassy track on the left to head north: this doubles back at first but then continues northwards to Bothwell Hill. Follow the track, always keeping the burn in sight on

the left side, to reach the corner of a fenced field. Now keep the fence to the left and climb alongside it to the top of the ridge where there is another fence and gate. Pass through the gate, and walk northwest along the rounded, heathery top of the ridge to join another grassy track and a gate towards the base of Spartleton. Beyond the gate, follow the track until it levels and then strike out across rough ground to the summit cairn and trig point (GR653655) (1h40). Descend southwards from the top towards the secretive ruins of Gamelshiel Castle. Cross the fence by a stile beside a burn to gain the castle. From the ruins, descend by a track above the burn to reach the northern arm of Whiteadder Reservoir. Turn left to follow the track down to the road, then turn right over the bridge and

◀ Whiteadder Reservoir

walk west for about 300m to a junction. Take the track on the left to follow the old Herring Road. Continue straight on at the next junction and cross a bridge to reach Priestlaw. After the first buildings, the gravel track turns north. Ignore this and continue east along a grassy track, passing through three gates. Follow the track uphill, ignoring a turning to the left down to the reservoir. Skirt above the plantation and

descend by the Friars' Nose. At the point where a fort is marked and just as the terrain steepens, watch for a stile on the left at the northeast tip of the fenced area. Cross this, and follow a path that descends through prickly gorse to another stile and down to the railings and parapets of the reservoir. Walk or roll down the embankment and cross the outflow by the bridges to reach the road and the start (3h20).

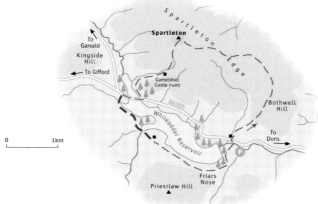

The packman's grave

The collection of stones by the side of the road at the Priestlaw to Garvald and Gifford junction is said to mark the grave of a packman who was murdered following a quarrel at a fair in Polwarth. From the 18th century until the early part of the 20th, packmen or 'tallymen' travelled the countryside selling clothes and other goods in return for small weekly payments, transporting their wares either on ponies or on their own backs and keeping a record of payment on a notched stick.

When the Romans came to conquer Scotland they were driven back by the harsh climate as well as by the local tribes. The remains of several of the roads they established to move troops and equipment, however, can still be seen running over these high, and frequently inhospitable, hills and many of the routes in this section follow in their footsteps.

The Cheviot moorland is the scene for four walks: Kirk Yetholm hosts the first and features part of the Pennine Way; the second tackles The Cheviot itself, and a third covers the rounded hills above Upper Coquetdale in Northumberland; the fourth lower route takes in the hills close to Morebattle, partly along St Cuthbert's Way. In the Langholm Hills there are two routes: the first begins in the Muckle Toon itself; the second visits more remote country near Hermitage Castle. The final route lies at the remote head of Ettrick Water: it overlooks the Moffat Hills but is best accessed from the south and east.

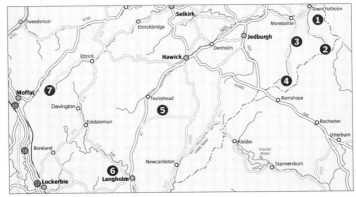

Cheviot and Langholm Hills

1   **Yetholm and the Black Hag**   82
Start in Scotland's Gypsy capital to slip through a hidden valley
in the English Cheviot and ascend Black Hag

2   **The Cheviot**   84
A cross-border adventure that follows the Pennine Way to climb
a lofty peak in remote land

3   **Morebattle Pilgrimage**   86
Lower hill walk that starts along St Cuthbert's Way and gives
a good viewpoint across frontier country

4   **Quiet as a Lamb**   88
Sneaky route that crosses the border, joins the Pennine Way
and passes an old fort. Good route-finding skills required

5   **Beyond Tudhope and Cauldcleuch**   90
Rough but interesting plateau deep in the Langholm Hills, with
a river crossing and some steep climbs to challenge

6   **The Muckle Toon Mountains**   92
Undulating route over two small sets of hills near Langholm with
a peaceful return through woodland above the River Esk

7   **Ettrick Views**   94
Remote setting for a climb over two peaks at the head of
Ettrick Water, with awesome views of the Moffat Hills

Yetholm and the Black Hag

Black Hag (549m)

Walk time 6h Height gain 19km
Distance 500m OS Map Landranger 74

An interesting route that begins by an historic pub to follow the end of the Pennine Way and other good paths and tracks into England.

Start by the Border Hotel on the village green in Kirk Yetholm (GR827282). From the green, walk southeast along the minor road, route of the Pennine Way/St Cuthbert's Way, and up the hill towards Halterburn. After descending to the glen, leave the road at a flat, grassy section and cross the burn by a footbridge. The long-distance footpaths climb alongside a wall and then rise gradually around Green Humbleton. When they split, continue southeast along the Pennine Way to reach a wall along the north ridge of White Law. Slink through a gate, and follow a path around the wide bowl: you have now left Scotland. Pass through a second gate to contour around Madam Law, which gives fine views of Black Hag, before a gentle descent takes you along the east ridge. At a walled enclosure, descend ESE to reach the farm at Trowupburn. Walk into the farmyard, turn right before a large barn and pass through two metal gates to access a track. This leads gently through a plantation and down

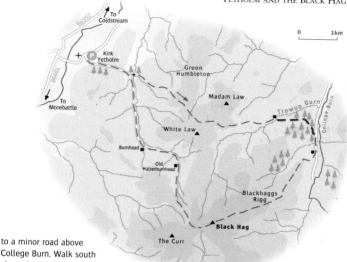

to a minor road above College Burn. Walk south along the road for about 800m to pass a house on the right. Leave the road after crossing the cattle grid to climb grassy slopes on the right and pick up the Hillfort Trail, which rises steeply to the remains of an old fort below Blackhaggs Rigg. Continue up the hill towards Black Hag: a vague grassy track hugs the south side of the ridge and gives easier walking over the boggy stretches. The highest point of the peak is close to a gate at the junction of three fences (GR862237) (4h). Pass through the gate and follow a fence northwest for 200m to reach a stile. Cross this to join the Pennine Way again. Descend to the bealach shared with The Curr and take the Pennine Way as it winds delightfully northwards. This avoids the farm at Burnhead by crossing the footbridge and following the wall before it joins the lower track. Continue along this and the road back to Kirk Yetholm (6h).

The Yetholm Gypsies

There are two differing accounts as to how Kirk Yetholm became the Gypsy capital of Scotland, both involving an act of kindness by a Romany traveller towards the local landowner who granted them land in gratitude. Whatever the origins, the village is home to what was the Gypsy Palace, which hosted the coronation in 1898 of the last King of the Gypsies, Charles Faa Blythe, and a more recent memorial stone on the village green.

◄ Trowup Burn and Loft Hill from Madam Law

83

The Cheviot

The Cheviot (815m)

Walk time 6h20 Height gain 600m
Distance 17km OS Map OL16

Good tracks lead to England where a paved route follows the border for some time with an optional detour to the highest hill in the area.

Start near the junction of minor roads that serve the farms of Sourhope and Cocklawfoot, by two weak bridges and two fords (GR840197). Walk southeast along the tarmac road to reach Cocklawfoot after 2km. Cross a bridge and enter the farmyard by a gate, exiting by another gate (under

large trees) on the right after about 30m. A grassy track leads you southeast, gaining height easily as it passes through a small plantation and winds its way up White Knowe and over The Bank to another gate. Pass through this, and climb to the top of the ridge at a stile and signposts. Cross into England and follow the Pennine Way northeast: once an arduous bog crossing, this impressive section has been tamed with huge blocks of stone. Follow the slabs over King's Seat and Score Head to reach duckboards and a junction. The raised trig point of The Cheviot is a 2km incursion into England, mostly on a good path but through

◄ The Cheviot from White Knowe

increasingly inhospitable terrain (GR908205) (4h20). Return to the junction. Continue northwest along the Pennine Way on duckboards, and descend the defined ridge that overlooks the wild chasm of Hen Hole. Climb slightly to gain the refuge. From this point, leave the Pennine Way by following the fenceline for about 200m to a convergence of fences, and pass through a gate. Drop southwest along Auchope Rig and follow the posts as the ground levels out and climbs again. When the fence turns away to the left, maintain your bearing and pass through a gate. Continue over undulating terrain and through another gate to reach the top of the old fort overlooking Sourhope. Rather than negotiate the complex walls to the west, descend north to reach a track and the farm buildings. Cross the river by the bridge and take the road back to the start (6h20).

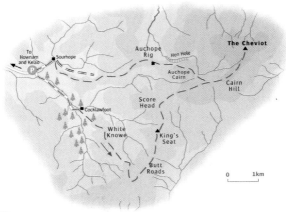

The Cheviot

The white-faced Cheviot ewe is known around the world for its ability to live off the hill throughout the year, even in the most severe conditions. Its durable wool, once the basis for the local Tweed industry, is today more commonly found in carpet manufacturing. In their early history, monks were primarily responsible for their upkeep as the Church owned much of the farmland and cattle were too easily plundered by Border reivers.

Morebattle Pilgrimage

Hownam Law (449m)

Walk time **4h** Height gain **450m**
Distance **10km** OS Map Landranger **74**

**A fine grassy ridge and good paths,
tracks and country lanes make for
an easygoing but occasionally
intricate circuit.**

Start in the village of Morebattle
(GR772248). Walk east down the road and
past the Templehall Hotel to a junction.
Turn right towards Hownam, climbing over a
steep hill to reach another road that winds
along the Kale Valley. Head south, and
watch for a footbridge over the Kale Water
after 600m. Cross this to follow a footpath
through the fields: this is St Cuthbert's Way,
linking Melrose Abbey with Lindisfarne.
The path takes you to a gateway and a
track, which should be followed for a
short way to open ground. From here,
climb alongside a small burn towards a
plantation. Cross a stile before the trees,
ford the burn and take a path alongside
the plantation wall to a higher stile. After
climbing this, bear eastwards over
rougher ground to reach Grubbit Law.
Ignore an intersecting grassy track and
instead follow the high ground to cross a
stile over a long snaking wall. This
descends southwards before climbing first
to Cushat End and then towards Hownam
Law. Cross the main dyke by a gate just
before an intersecting wall, and pass

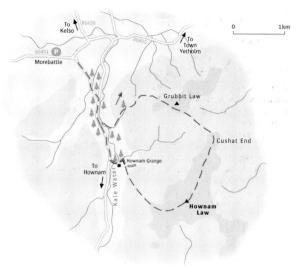

through this second dyke by another gate. Rough heathery slopes lead to the summit of Hownam Law, where there is a trig point but little evidence of the ancient fort (GR797219) (3h). Descend steeply southwest by the sharp nose of Grange Hill to gentler ground at the corner of a wall. Go through the gate just beyond and take a grassy track northwest. Pass through another gate, skirting around the edge of a large field to descend to the farm buildings of Hownam Grange. A gate gives access to the farm road, which zigzags down to meet the road beside the Kale Water. Walk north and retrace your steps to the start (4h).

Hill forts

Hownam Law is thought to be named after the Hunas, the Iron Age people who built their hill fort here. There are estimated to be around 20,000 hill fort sites in Europe, of which some 1000 are in Scotland, their settlement dating from the late Bronze Age, about 2000BC, through to Roman times. Traprain Law in East Lothian is the largest surviving hill fort in Scotland, although Edinburgh and Stirling Castles also occupy what would have been commanding sites.

◀ Hownam Law from St Cuthbert's Way

Quiet as a Lamb

Lamb Hill (511m)

Walk time 4h20 Height gain 300m
Distance 15km OS Map Landranger 80

Good navigation skills are a must for this varied circuit in the Cheviots with its mix of good tracks, mountain paths and difficult, boggy ground.

Start at Tow Ford over Kale Water, 6.5km south of Hownam (GR760133). On the east side of the road junction, you will see a stile: climb this to join a path which leads you across a field, over a second stile and southeast up a gentle incline. After 400m, near some sheep pens, the path widens to a grassy track and leads up to a bealach by a square building. From this point you can see much of the route, which traverses the far skyline. Continue along the track towards Blackhall Hill until, close to the top, the track diverges. Rather than

passing through the gate (marked for Dere Street, a Roman Road), take the left branch to pass near the top of the hill. Head northeast by rough tracks over almost featureless ground towards Rushy (Raeshaw) Fell. Instead of climbing the knoll, strike across the quaggy mire of Broad Flow and slip unnoticed across the border fence by a gate. The Pennine Way lies just beyond. Follow this northeast over well-laid slabs to a refuge, and then up to Lamb Hill (easiest keeping close to the fence) and a trig point (GR810133) (2h). Continue on the Pennine Way to an abrupt rightwards kink in the fence, halfway to the top of Beefstand Hill. Leave the path here and go through a gate to follow the northwest ridge. A simple path takes you beneath the north side of Callaw to a small gate. Pass through this and climb to the summit with its large

Fort above Yett Burn, near Tow Ford ▲

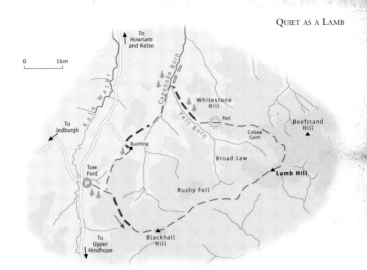

cairn. Drop westwards on tracks and paths
to reach the fort below Whitestone Hill: its
triple ditch and spiralling walls give a
dominating perspective over the glen.
Descend west to then follow the track
alongside Yett Burn for about 1km, and cut
across rough ground to the end of a line of
trees at an intersection of walls. Jump over
two burns and pass through two stiles to
join a rugged path southwards, keeping
height above Capehope Burn. This path
becomes a track, meandering up the glen to

reach a tarmac road below the farm of
Buchtrig. Turn left, cross the cattle grid and
follow the private road towards the farm.
Take the first track on the right after 150m,
pass through one gate and then, after
300m, another gate into a large field.
Rather than climb up through the field, drop
slightly to a fence above a small reservoir.
Follow this fence to reach a grassy track.
This leads easily southwards to the path by
the sheep pens, leaving only a short
distance back to the start (4h20).

What the Romans did

The Roman road known as Dere Street was constructed in the late 1st century AD to link
the legionary fortress of York (Eburacum) and Inchtuthil, near Perth. In total there were
over 53,000 miles (85,000km) of road built by the Romans in Britain and Europe to enable
troop movement and trade, although much of it fell into disuse as their empire declined.
Dere Street was later adopted as a drove road and several parts of it were overlain by the
A1 and A68.

Beyond Tudhope and Cauldcleuch

Tudhope Hill (599m),
Cauldcleuch Head (619m)

Walk time 5h20 Height gain 700m
Distance 15km OS Map Landranger 79

Multiple peaks with plenty of ascent, sections of bog and spectacular views over the surrounding hills make this a well-rewarded challenge. The return along the burn may be difficult in spate.

Start at a parking area by the bridge over the Carewoodrighope Burn, about 2km from the A7, on the minor road to Hermitage Castle (GR411969). Climb directly north from the parking bay. Rough ground leads to a vague ridge and a cairn, marking the southwest top of Ellson Fell. Follow the grassy ridge northeast over the fell and small bumps beyond. After passing another cairn, join the edge of a fence which can be easily followed to Carlin Tooth. Descend steeply northeast to a bealach where there is a path and gate. [Escape: descend southeast along a path above Carewoodrighope Burn and down to the road.] Continue along the fence to the summit of Tudhope Hill, achieved by two tough climbs (GR431992) (2h20). Follow the fence along the northeast ridge over increasingly savage ground to Millstone Edge, with no distinguishing marks but the meeting point of three fences. Pass through the gate here, and follow the eastbound fence over peaty undulations and around to the unmarked summit of Cauldcleuch Head. Rather than follow the main ridge south,

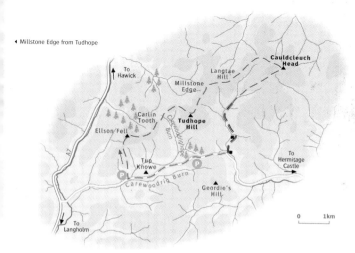

◀ Millstone Edge from Tudhope

start to drop southwest on terrain that immediately improves. Descend over North Mid Hill to the confluence of two burns at an old ruin. Follow the water downstream to soon join the end of a track. This crosses and re-crosses Billhope Burn several times and, where the burn switches south, the track climbs away from the water for a short while before meandering gradually down the glen. Avoid the first house by passing through two gates on its left side. From here, it is only a short walk to Billhope and the road. Climb westwards over the brow of the hill (alternative parking at the forest entrance) and amble gently back to the start (5h20).

Hermitage Castle

Hermitage is said to be haunted by the spirit of the very nasty Sir Nicholas de Soules, builder of the first wooden castle on the site in 1242 and practitioner of the black arts. Held responsible for the disappearance of several children, he was, according to legend, captured by angry locals who then boiled him in a brass cauldron at the top of a nearby hill. The castle is also associated with Mary Queen of Scots, who rode straight from Edinburgh to tend to a wounded Bothwell here and spent ten days in bed recovering afterwards as a result, and Sir Walter Scott, whose interest caused Hermitage to be repaired sufficiently for it to survive until it was taken into state care in the 1930s.

The Muckle Toon Mountains

Black Knowe (326m),
Crumpton Hill (480m)

Walk time 6h40 Height gain 600m
Distance 22km OS Map Landranger 79

An intricate route with rough tracks and demanding heathery slopes rewarded by great views. This circuit can easily be divided into two shorter walks.

Start at the Langholm Parish Church on the west bank of the River Esk (GR361845). (Car park just north of the town.) Walk west along Caroline Street, and cross the footbridge on the left to enter the park behind the church. Skirt around the back of the park and up the steps in the wood to a dirt track. Turn right and follow Gaskells Walk above the Wauchope Water to the road where you should turn right again,

cross the bridge and take the minor road on the left after 130m. This leads to a T-junction at a farm. Turn left onto the track and follow this for 1km until a metal gate takes you out to the open fell. Leave the track here, and walk north along a wall. Where this kinks to the east, climb over Calfield Rig instead. Follow the undulations northwards and a wall further on to the top of Black Knowe (GR334859) (2h20). Drop north to a bealach and go through a gate in the wall. Descend next to a plantation and through a second gate to reach a track, which leads easily down to the road. Walk north and take the junction on the right after 200m. Follow the minor road for Hawick downhill, crossing the River Esk by a bridge. [Escape: turn right after the bridge

◄ East towards Langholm from Calfield Rig

and take the Hawick road for about 2km to reach the track for Potholm.] Turn left to follow a track, bearing right at the fork to reach a farmhouse about 400m from the bridge. Take the main track on the right which doubles back and then switches back again to continue northwest through a plantation. Exit the trees by a gate and swing west to find a gate on the right after 100m. Pass through this and take a grassy track that shadows Back Burn and leads to the far northern tip of the plantation. Go through a gate to access the uncompromising heathery slopes that lead to the top of Crumpton Hill (GR346914) (4h40).

Cross to the north side of the fence and descend southwards, following the edge of the plantation over rough terrain, to reach a bealach with two gates under Bauchle Hill. Pass through the second of these and climb diagonally to the dip between Bauchle Hill and Golf Hill. Descend southwards and cross the burn to reach the minor Hawick Road at a gate. Go directly over the road where there is a farm track to Potholm. After 1km, the track descends towards the collection of houses. Take the first turn on the left that serves both a fine residence and a track above: this leads south through mixed woodland. Ignore any minor turns as it takes you through Langfauld Wood to Holmhead. A tree-lined avenue leads to a bridge over the Ewes Water and the Muckle Toon of Langholm (6h40).

Ettrick Views

Bodesbeck Law (665m),
Capel Fell (678m)

Walk time 4h Height gain 500m
Distance 11km OS Map Landranger 79

A half-day circuit which follows a rounded ridge to climb two hills. This route contains some boggy ground but no major navigation difficulties, with easy tracks in access and return.

Start at the end of the public road along the Ettrick Water, 9km southwest of the village of Ettrick (GR188093). (Better parking 800m northeast.) Take the track that climbs westwards into the forest. Ignore a fork that crosses Longhope Burn, and instead climb gently towards Bught Hill. Where the track fades after exiting the forest, continue on grassy slopes over Bught Hill to reach Bodesbeck Law. The plateau is a mass of folds and dips, and access to the very top is obstructed by the high county wall. Follow this wall and drop southeast to a wide bealach, passing through a gate to reach a track. [Escape: follow the track eastwards and around Pot Law to the start.] Cross the county boundary by another gate on the right and tramp across heathery